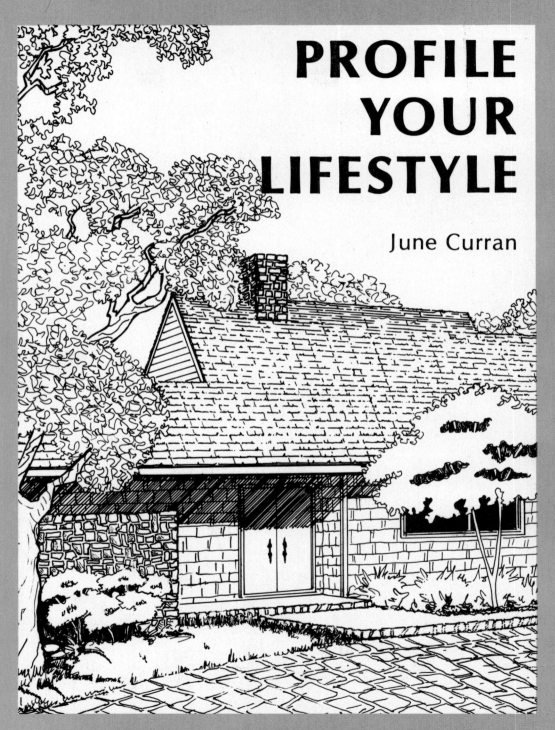

PROFILE YOUR LIFESTYLE

June Curran

Questions To Ask Yourself Before
Building, Buying, or Remodeling

PROFILE
YOUR
LIFESTYLE

PROFILE YOUR LIFESTYLE

Questions To Ask Yourself Before Building, Buying, or Remodeling

JUNE CURRAN

Registered Building Designer
Member American Institute of Building Design

Cover Illustration by
June Curran

Brooks Publishing Company
930 Truxtun Ave., Suite 210
Bakersfield, CA 93301

BROOKS

Life Enrichment Through Knowledge And Action

Brooks Publishing Company titles are distributed worldwide by William Kaufmann, Inc., Los Altos, California. For further information regarding distribution outside of the United States of America, write to Foreign Sales Department, William Kaufmann, Inc., One First Street, Los Altos, CA 94022.

10   9   8   7   6   5   4   3   2   1

Library of Congress Cataloging in Publication Data

Curran, June
   Profile your lifestyle.

1. House construction—Handbooks, manuals, etc.
2. Dwellings—Remodeling—Handbooks, manuals, etc.
3. House buying—Handbooks, manuals, etc. I. Title.
TH4813.C87   643   78-72187
ISBN 0-932370-00-4

The Supervising Editor for this book was Ruth Weine. It was typeset in Oracle by Roberta Bowen, B.R.S. Type House. Printed by Banta Book System in the U.S.A.

ACKNOWLEDGMENTS

Thanks to Nancy Giumarra, Shay Wilbur, Evanell Yelich, Bonnie Jones, and Sueanne Gladney for their invaluable assistance in the preparation of this material. Thanks also, to my husband, Hugh Curran, for the inspiration and encouragement he contributes to each of my writing ventures.

TABLE OF CONTENTS

SECTION 4

MAKING FINAL DECISIONS AND WRITING YOUR OWN SPECIFICATIONS — 139

PREFACE

This self-discovery book provides the means for focusing your ideas and energies on your priority requirements in a home. It guides you in the process of exploring your feelings and discovering your needs, and it is the first step toward solving your housing problems.

The lifestyle-evaluation process presented here can be an individual effort; or it can be a family* project, but the home you plan will be a reflection of you — your personality, your philosophy, your way of life. Whether you are planning to build or modify a single-family house, a condominium, a mobile home, an apartment, or a houseboat, the spaces behind the outer facade will reflect the inner you.

A significant aspect of my work as a building designer is getting to know the individuals for whom I'm designing, so that they can help me plan the right home for them, one that will fit their own unique lifestyle. Because it isn't always possible for a designer to know a client truly well, I wrote out a list of questions for people to answer about themselves before I started work on their plans — questions that defined their desires and their needs. And that is what this book is all about.

I have developed a procedure for your participation in this all-important first phase of home planning and I would like to share it with you. It makes little difference whether you will be doing your own work or working with a design professional, because this material embodies decisions that you will want to make for yourself.

When you have completed your lifestyle profile, and each person who is, or will be, living in the home has had an opportunity to express personal views and consolidated them into a workable plan, you will have a blueprint which is an illuminating reflection of your lifestyle. Then, when the time comes for you to build, remodel, or buy a home, you can proceed without hesitation, secure in the knowledge that your decisions are based on sound reasoning that takes into account the needs of each individual involved. Moreover, you will have a home that is both a true reflection of the planning you have put into it and a joy to live in.

You may just find that the process of sharing ideas and priorities will stimulate your thinking and broaden the lines of personal communication. You are bound to discover a great deal about yourself — and each other — through this give-and-take process of evaluating your housing needs and establishing your priorities.

June Curran

*The family or family unit, as referred to in this lifestyle profile is meant to include everyone sharing the home, whether the family is the traditional one, or consists of individuals sharing common facilities.

HOW TO USE THIS BOOK

Defining your lifestyle for the purpose of planning a home for yourself and/or your family is a very personal thing — and this book will become very personal to you. Use it as a lifestyle analysis and planning guide. Write in it! Express your feelings, emotions, and desires. Jot down ideas and mark it up to suit yourself. Each person who will be sharing the home should have an opportunity to express personal ideas and preferences.

I have attempted to leave enough writing space for this, but if you need more space for all your thoughts and plans, use a notebook to supplement the pages.

Most of the choices and questions call for more than a *yes* or *no* answer, and the alternatives listed represent only a few of the possibilities. The ruled lines and pages in each section are for your ideas and decisions. Have family members express themselves freely *in the book*. This is the time to create, brainstorm, forget restraints, and collaborate. Remember that *because I like it* is often a justifiable position.

Before the last section is written and final choices are made, some of the ideas you have gained from freedom of expression may become priorities. In the final analysis, *trade-offs* will be inevitable. You will sometimes have to sacrifice one idea to accommodate another — or to accommodate the budget. But you will be making conscious, positive choices.

Eventually the process of home planning resolves itself into one of product selection; the satisfaction you will gain from your home is dependent to a large measure on the selections you make. To make wise choices, you will need information. The following suggestions will help you to make informed decisions.

• Send for the manufacturers' literature listed in shelter or home magazines. Often it is free, or at least very inexpensive. Although this literature is designed to sell products, it can provide you with a treasure of information and usually proves to be a real bargain.

• Visit dealers' displays of building materials, appliances, plumbing and electrical fixtures, etc. While you are there, pick up the pamphlets they have to offer.

• Go through model homes. It is not necessary to contact real estate agents to do this; most developers welcome drop-in guests.

• Buy as many home-planning idea books and magazines as you can afford, or get them from your library. There are hundreds of these publications available in every price range, and many contain creative ideas that can also save you money.

• Consult SOURCES OF SUPPLEMENTARY INFORMATION in the back of this book for a list of helpful books and publications.

• Organize the material you collect for handy reference. Folders and notebooks are convenient for this purpose.

As your planning progresses, you will begin to make some definite decisions. Record them carefully in SECTION 4, MAKING FINAL DECISIONS AND WRITING YOUR OWN SPECIFICATIONS. This section is designed to be used for listing final choices. It will be your guide when you are designing your project. When SECTION 4 is finalized, the pages can be removed from the book and copied, then handed to the people who will be working with you in the areas of design, cost estimating, and construction. With well-defined specifications, you can be sure that you are actually getting the items you have chosen — thus avoiding errors, delays, substitutions, and misunderstandings during construction.

SECTION

1

FACTORS THAT INFLUENCE YOUR LIFESTYLE

The lifestyle of each individual or each family unit develops from a combination of factors. Personal goals, values, careers, recreation, and monetary resources all play a part. SECTION 1 of this lifestyle profile focuses on some of the many factors that affect the lives of each of the members of a household.

Since life is rarely static, the most effective planning is done by those who think in terms of the future as well as the present. So before you begin your planning, gaze into your crystal ball and try to visualize your home/life situation in five, or even ten years from now. The goal should be a plan for a home that will suit your needs in the future as well as it will today.

THE SIZE OF YOUR FAMILY

When deciding on the floor space and the number of rooms needed in a home, one usually takes into account the number of people the house must accommodate. It is important, therefore, for you to consider the size of your family, not only as it is to-day but also as it may be in the future.

Most families must also consider the number of overnight guests they expect to entertain in their homes. For example, friends and/or relatives who may spend weekends or even weeks in your home, or your children's school friends who may spend the night.

Your answers to the following questions will help in determining the amount of floor space and the number of rooms your family actually needs.

1. *HOW MANY FAMILY MEMBERS MUST YOUR HOME ACCOMMODATE?*

   Adults living at home:

      Full-time _____ *Part-time* _____

   Children living at home:

      Full-time _____ *Ages* _____

      Part-time _____ *Ages* _____

      Summers and holidays _____ *Weekends* _____

2. *WILL THE SIZE OF YOUR FAMILY BE CHANGING?* _____

   _____

3. *WILL ANYONE BE LEAVING HOME FOR COLLEGE, WORK, OR MARRIAGE*

   WITHIN THE NEXT FIVE YEARS? _____

4. *WILL YOU NEED SLEEPING ACCOMMODATIONS FOR GUESTS WHO STAY*

   Overnight? _____

   For a weekend? _____

   For long periods of time? _____

COMMENTS AND REMINDERS: _____

_____

CAREER GOALS AND JOB-RELATED ACTIVITIES

Your career goals, your present job, and activities that relate to your work are all strong factors in the formulation of individual lifestyles; they usually influence your decisions about such things as the city in which you live, the type of home you choose, your friends, and the way you entertain.

In homes where more than one person is pursuing a career, this factor becomes increasingly significant; it often affects the way you manage your household and the way your children are reared.

The questions in this section of your lifestyle profile will alert you to the strong relationship between careers and job-related activities and the way you live in a home.

1. *IN WHAT WAYS DO THE CAREERS OR JOB-RELATED ACTIVITIES OF FAMILY MEMBERS AFFECT THE FOLLOWING THINGS?*

   Lifestyle:

   Where you live _____

   _____

   Your leisure time _____

   _____

   The way you entertain _____

   _____

   The kind of house you will need _____

   _____

   Your future plans _____

   _____

   Housekeeping and Maintaining Your Home:

   The number of household tasks each of you must perform _____

   _____

The need to employ household help _____

_____

The need to employ a babysitter _____

_____

The number of jobs sent out to be done _____

_____

The division of gardening chores _____

_____

The need to employ gardening and/or maintenance help _____

_____

2. IF ANYONE IN THE FAMILY WORKS DURING OTHER THAN DAYTIME HOURS, HOW DOES THIS AFFECT THE FOLLOWING THINGS?

Your domestic routine _____

_____

Your mealtimes _____

_____

Other members' free or activity time _____

_____

Space arrangements in your home _____

_____

_____

_____

_____

Each of you should now describe the way in which your job or job-related activities affect you and the other members of the household in relation to your housing needs. List ways in which better space arrangements could alleviate problems resulting from any of the things previously listed. Also list any facilities, storage arrangements, etc., needed by family member(s) who work(s) at home.

_____

_____

_____

_____

_____

COMMENTS AND REMINDERS: _____

_____

_____

_____

_____

_____

_____

_____

_____

_____

_____

_____

_____

RECREATION AND AVOCATIONS

Another facet of your life that often exerts equal impact on your lifestyle and your requirements in a home is the diverse ways in which family members use their leisure time. Some individuals choose active sports of one form or another, others enjoy hobbies such as collecting things, craft projects, sewing, woodworking, etc. Often parents engage in activities that involve the entire family, such as camping, boating, or skiing.

Recreational interests frequently develop into avocations or business sidelines. Special facilities are often needed in the home to accommodate such avocations as photography, artwork, sculpture, jewelry making, small business ventures, and a host of others.

Your answers to the following questions will help to clarify any special space, storage, or display requirements you may have in this regard.

1. *IN THIS SPACE, EACH FAMILY MEMBER SHOULD LIST HIS OR HER OWN LEISURE-TIME ACTIVITIES.* _____

_____

_____

_____

_____

_____

2. *WILL YOU NEED A SPECIAL ROOM OR ALCOVE IN THE HOUSE FOR THE PROJECTS OF ANY FAMILY MEMBER(S)?* _____

_____

_____

_____

_____

3. *WILL YOU NEED A CORNER OF THE GARAGE FOR A SHOP?* _____

4. *WILL YOU NEED STORAGE FACILITIES FOR ANY OF THE FOLLOWING?*

A boat _____   *A camper* _____

Camping, hunting, or fishing equipment _____

Athletic equipment _____

Supplies and/or equipment for hobbies or crafts:

     Collections _____

     Trophies _____

     Books _____

     Other _____

5. WHAT AREA OF THE HOUSE OR GARAGE WOULD BE MOST CONVENIENT AND LOGICAL FOR STORAGE OF ANY OF THESE ITEMS? _____

_____

_____

6. LIST ANY OTHER STORAGE OR SPACE REQUIREMENTS YOU HAVE THAT ARE RELEVANT TO RECREATION AND/OR AVOCATIONS. _____

_____

_____

_____

COMMENTS AND REMINDERS: _____

_____

_____

_____

_____

_____

_____

_____

_____

PHYSICAL CHARACTERISTICS OF INDIVIDUAL FAMILY MEMBERS

In the interest of simplifying construction procedures and keeping costs under control, manufacturers of building materials, supplies, fixtures, and equipment have adopted sizes and measurements that are proportioned for the *average* person. Workers in each of the building crafts are trained to work efficiently within these standards.

There are many important things achieved by standardization, but it does create special problems for persons whose physical characteristics cannot be defined as *average* — persons who are taller, shorter, larger, or smaller for example.

Taller persons, living in homes constructed to industry standards, must frequently stoop or bend their bodies awkwardly to perform the simplest functions in their homes. Short persons are forever dragging stools around to reach items on the shelves of cupboards that are too high or working at counters far too high for comfort. Large persons have difficulty fitting themselves comfortably into tiny bathrooms, small bathtubs and showers, narrow hallways, and many other small places. Those persons who are not mobile, or who require special equipment — such as wheelchairs, walkers, or crutches — find industry standards almost impossible to live with.

To build a house with features that deviate from standards is not necessarily more costly. It can be achieved by adapting standard materials in imaginative ways. This calls for careful advance planning and attention to details during construction.

If you do not indicate clearly on your plans and in your specifications what your special requirements are, things will automatically be done in the standard way. So take time now to think about any special or nonstandard requirements that are important to you.

One should also consider, when making major changes that deviate from standards, that these changes could have a negative effect on the resale value of the home.

KITCHEN CABINETS

Special requirements can easily be filled if cabinets are custom made, but this can be costly. More often cabinets are selected from those offered by cabinet manufacturers. These cabinets will be constructed to industry standards. The following information applies to manufactured cabinets.

The cabinets beneath the counter, called base cabinets, are usually 35 inches high. When the counter top has been installed, the height from the floor to the top of the counter is 36 inches. There is a 4-inch toe-strip allowance at the base of the cabinets. This can be trimmed to lower them. It is also possible to raise cabinets by placing them on blocks.

1. WILL YOU NEED CABINETS THAT ARE

Lower than standard? _____ *By how many inches?* _____

Higher than standard? _____ *By how many inches?* _____

Wall cabinets come in many widths and heights but they are usually mounted on the wall at a level approximately 18 inches above the counter top.

2. WILL YOU NEED CABINETS THAT ARE MOUNTED ON THE WALL AT A LEVEL

Lower than standard? _____ *By how many inches?* _____

Higher than standard? _____ *By how many inches?* _____

BATHROOM VANITIES AND BASINS

Bathroom basins are usually installed in cabinets (often called vanities) that measure 30 to 32 inches from the floor to the top of the basin. Depths (measurements from front to back) of counter tops vary from approximately 18 inches to 24 inches.

3. WILL YOU NEED A VANITY AND BASIN THAT IS INSTALLED

Lower than standard? _____ *By how many inches?* _____

Higher than standard? _____ *By how many inches?* _____

4. IS IT IMPORTANT TO YOU THAT THE VANITY COUNTER TOP BE

The maximum depth? _____ *Generously long?* _____

BATHTUBS AND GRAB BARS

A standard bathtub is 60 inches in length and is usually 30 inches in depth (from front to back) although some of the newer models are 2 or 3 inches deeper. The standard height (measurement from floor to top) is 16 inches. Bathtubs are manufactured in a variety of special sizes and shapes, but the standard 60-inch tub is the least expensive. A grab bar (piece of chromed pipe installed near bathtubs for use by those who need something to grasp when getting in and out of a bathtub) should be installed if needed.

5. DESCRIBE IN THIS SPACE ANY SPECIAL REQUIREMENTS IN SIZE OR SHAPE

OF BATHTUB OR GRAB BARS YOU MAY HAVE. _____

_____

_____

ELBOW ROOM

6. *DO YOU NEED MORE SPACE THAN IS USUALLY ALLOWED TO MOVE ABOUT*

   In your kitchen? _____ *In your bathroom?* _____ *In other rooms?* _____

7. *DESCRIBE ANY SPECIAL SPACE REQUIREMENTS RELATED TO PHYSICAL CHARACTERISTICS OF INDIVIDUALS.* _____

   _____

   _____

   _____

   _____

   _____

   _____

BEDS

If any family member(s) need(s) a bed that is longer than the average 72 to 74 inches, this should be taken into account when planning bedrooms.

8. *WILL YOU NEED BED(S) LONGER THAN AVERAGE?* _____

   _____

HALLS

The measurement considered standard for hallways (other than the entry) is 3 feet between walls. This width is usually adequate unless you are a large person or, for mobility, require special equipment.

9. *DO YOU NEED HALLWAYS THAT ARE*

   Wider than standard? _____

   How much wider should they be? _____

ELECTRICAL OUTLETS AND SWITCHES

Electrical outlets are usually installed at a height approximately 12 inches up from the floor, and switches are placed 50 inches up unless otherwise indicated on the plan. These heights are sometimes inconvenient for persons in wheel chairs or with other special requirements. Electrical outlets and switches can be installed at any height you desire and at no extra cost, simply by marking the desired height of each on the plan presented to the electrician.

10. *LIST ANY SPECIAL REQUIREMENTS YOU MAY HAVE FOR ELECTRICAL OUTLETS AND SWITCHES.* _____

_____

RAMPS AND/OR RAILINGS

11. *WILL YOU NEED RAMPS OR RAILINGS AT THE ENTRANCE(S) TO YOUR HOME?* _____

    IF SO, DESCRIBE YOUR REQUIREMENTS. _____

_____

12. *IF YOU HAVE ANY OTHER REQUIREMENTS PERTINENT TO THE SPECIAL PHYSICAL CHARACTERISTICS OF ANY FAMILY MEMBER(S), DESCRIBE THEM HERE.* _____

_____

_____

_____

_____

COMMENTS AND REMINDERS: _____

_____

_____

_____

_____

_____

_____

HOW YOU RELATE TO SPACE

Each of us experiences space in a different way. Some people delight in rooms that are flooded with light and sunshine and enjoy an airy, spacious atmosphere in a home. This effect can often be achieved, even in a small home, through design of a plan that incorporates wide expanses of glass and that permits one area to flow into another visually.

The reverse spatial concept is equally significant. Many of us opt for living spaces divided into cheerful, cozy, inward-looking rooms, often with windows that are smaller than average and that are screened or draped for privacy. A very restful, intimate, and homelike feeling can be attained by treating small spaces individually. The goal here would be to create nooks and retreats for the personal use of individual family members.

But spatial relationships are not easy to deal with when one recognizes that different family members may relate to space in distinctly different ways. A planning solution to this type of problem might be to design a home in which major living areas open to an interior garden or incorporate a view. Then one can allow space for an inviting den or cozy family room. Bedrooms should be designed according to the preferences of those who will occupy them.

Answers to the following questions will help you to analyze your interior space requirements from the viewpoint of each member of your family.

OUTWARD-LOOKING INTERIOR SPACES

1. *DO YOU PREFER LIVING SPACES THAT*

   Flow together? _____

   Open visually to a garden or view? _____

   Have an airy, spacious feeling? _____

2. *SHOULD YOUR ROOMS*

   Incorporate wide expanses of glass? _____

   Open to deck, patio, terrace, or porch? _____

   Have windows that incorporate or frame a view? _____

   Have sheer draperies through which light can filter? _____

   Be furnished with pieces that are light and small in scale? _____

   Have some built-in furniture? _____

INWARD-LOOKING SPACES

3. *DO YOU PREFER TO HAVE MOST OF THE FLOOR SPACE IN YOUR HOME DIVIDED INTO INDIVIDUAL ROOMS THAT CAN BE CLOSED OFF?* _____

4. *WOULD YOU LIKE TO CREATE A COZY, INTIMATE FEELING IN YOUR HOME?* _____

5. *WOULD YOU LIKE YOUR WINDOWS TO BE*

   Average in size? _____

   The minimum size required by building codes? _____

   Draped or screened for privacy? _____

OUTWARD- AND INWARD-LOOKING SPACES

6. *DO YOU PREFER THAT YOUR HOME HAVE SOME OPEN SPACES AND OTHERS THAT ARE COZY AND PRIVATE?* _____

7. *IN WHICH ROOMS WOULD YOU LIKE TO CREATE AN OPEN FEELING?* _____

   _____

8. *WHICH ROOMS SHOULD BE OPEN TO EACH OTHER?* _____

9. *WHICH ROOMS SHOULD BE OPEN TO THE GARDEN, TERRACE, PATIO, OR DECK?* _____

10. *WHICH ROOMS SHOULD HAVE THE MOST INTIMATE AND PRIVATE ATMOSPHERE?* _____

    _____

COMMENTS AND REMINDERS: _____

_____

_____

_____

_____

INDIVIDUAL NEED FOR PRIVACY

A space of one's own is such a necessary thing — and so hard to find in the average home. Because of the ever-increasing cost of obtaining living space, trends in architecture are toward more open, communal areas. An illusion of spaciousness is created when limited space is expanded visually. Although a delightful atmosphere can be achieved by using this design concept, much needed privacy is often sacrificed.

Adequate areas of space for interaction between family members and friends are inherent in the design of most homes, but one also needs a place to withdraw from the group — to be alone with one's thoughts. When such private spaces are not available in the home, people find other ways to create a sense of solitude or to ward off intrusion into their private worlds. Watching sports events on television, listening to stereo music — sometimes using a headset for further isolation — reading, studying, are but a few.

Even when parents are able to provide separate bedrooms for their small children and/or young adults, they rarely have individual privacy for themselves. Since it is assumed, by custom, that a couple will share facilities, most find it difficult to break with convention and physically divide their common space or to reveal to one another their need for privacy.

All too often, the bathroom is the only inviolate space in the house, and possesses the only door with a lock.

Some innovative people do manage to create a place *where one is not to be disturbed* for each family member, even when the size of the house is limited and the family is large. This can often be achieved through careful, creative planning and by examining all possibilities. Sometimes unconventional solutions work very well.

The questions that follow will give you some ideas about creating privacy for individuals. Some clues may be discovered if you refer back to each person's list under "Recreation and Avocations."

1. WILL YOU BE ABLE TO PROVIDE SEPARATE BEDROOMS WHERE NEEDED?

_____

2. IF NOT, CONSIDER SOME OF THESE IDEAS.

For Young Children or Teen-agers:

Bunk beds and storage units or screens in bedrooms to create visual privacy

_____

_____

A portion of the garage for working on projects _____

A bunk house or play house in the back yard _____

A tree house or fort _____

Other arrangement(s)

_____

For Adults:

A furniture grouping that will create a secluded reading or studying area

_____

Plants or screens that divide areas _____

_____

Other ideas to visually separate space _____

_____

_____

3. IF YOU ARE REMODELING, IS THERE A SPACE THAT COULD BE CONVERTED FOR USE AS A PRIVATE RETREAT, SUCH AS

A seldom-used dining room? _____

A butler's pantry? _____

A front or back porch? _____

An attic space? _____

Some other space? _____

4. COULD YOU CREATE PRIVATE SPACES IN THE GARDEN BY BUILDING

A greenhouse? _____

A summerhouse? _____

A barn or screened area for the owner of animals or pets? _____

_____

Some other structure(s)? _____

_____

5. LIST ANY OTHER IDEAS YOU MAY HAVE FOR INDIVIDUAL PRIVACY.

_____

_____

_____

6. DO FAMILY MEMBERS KNOCK ON CLOSED DOORS BEFORE ENTERING?

_____

7. IF NOT, SHOULD SOME INTERIOR DOORS BE EQUIPPED WITH LOCKS?

_____

8. LIST THE DOORS ON WHICH YOU WOULD LIKE TO HAVE LOCKS.

_____

_____

COMMENTS AND REMINDERS: _____

_____

_____

_____

_____

_____

_____

_____

_____

_____

THE INDOOR GARDENER

If there is someone in your family who has joined the legion of indoor plant-lovers, be warned! This is a fascination that grows on one, and it is best to make provisions in your planning for growing, displaying and caring for plants.

GROWING PLANTS

1. WOULD YOU LIKE SPECIAL INDOOR WORKSPACE FOR POTTING AND TRANSPLANTING? _____

2. SHOULD YOUR WORKSPACE HAVE

   A sink? _____

   A built-in work counter? _____

   Storage space for pots, potting soil, fertilizers, and supplies? _____

3. WHERE SHOULD THESE FACILITIES BE LOCATED? _____

   _____

4. COULD THE UTILITY AREA SERVE A DUAL PURPOSE? _____

5. IF A GREENHOUSE FIGURES IN YOUR PLANS, WHERE SHOULD IT BE LOCATED? _____

6. DESCRIBE THE SPECIAL FEATURES IT SHOULD HAVE.

   Heating _____

   Lighting _____

   Water from a tap or hose _____

   A sink _____

   Other _____

   _____

   _____

   _____

DISPLAYING PLANTS

7. IN WHAT ROOMS DO YOU PLAN TO DISPLAY PLANTS? _____

    _____

8. WILL YOU WANT SPECIAL SUNNY OR SHADED WINDOWS FOR THEM?

    _____

9. WOULD YOU WANT TO GROW PLANTS ON A SHELTERED DECK OR PATIO?

    _____

    _____

CARING FOR PLANTS

10. ARE THERE ANY SPECIAL PROVISIONS YOU WOULD LIKE TO MAKE FOR

    PLANT CARE? _____

    _____

11. THIS SPACE IS RESERVED FOR THE PLANT PERSON(S) IN THE FAMILY. WRITE

    DOWN ALL OF YOUR OWN IDEAS AND PLANS FOR INDOOR GARDENING.

    _____

    _____

    _____

    _____

    _____

    _____

    _____

    _____

    _____

    _____

    _____

PROVISIONS FOR PETS

Pets come in all sizes, shapes, and varieties, i.e., furred, finned, feathered, and others. Each requires its own habitat. If yours is a pet-loving, pet-acquiring family, you will need to make some pet provisions and decisions while your home is in the planning stage. By making plans for pets in advance, you can minimize the negative aspects of owning and caring for them, and have more time to enjoy them.

In most communities there are regulatory laws pertaining to pets. It would be wise to investigate local ordinances while your project is in the planning stages and before purchasing land or a home.

INDOOR PETS

1. *WHAT KIND OF PET(S) DO YOU HAVE NOW OR PLAN TO HAVE IN THE FUTURE?* _____

2. *WILL YOU WANT A PET DOOR THAT YOUR ANIMAL CAN USE TO GO IN AND OUT OF THE HOUSE?* _____

3. *IF SO, WHERE SHOULD IT BE LOCATED?* _____

4. *WHERE WILL YOUR PET(S) BE FED?* _____

5. *ARE PETS TO BE RESTRICTED FROM ANY PARTICULAR AREA OF THE HOUSE?*

   _____

6. *WILL YOU NEED A PLACE TO BATHE YOUR PET?* _____

7. *WILL YOU WANT A SPECIAL RUN, CAGE, OR OTHER FACILITY OUTDOORS?*

   _____

OUTDOOR PETS

8. *WHAT KIND OF OUTDOOR PETS DO YOU HAVE OR PLAN TO HAVE?*

   _____

9. *WHAT SPECIAL FACILITIES WILL BE NEEDED ON YOUR LOT FOR THESE PETS?*

   _____

   _____

10. *USE THIS SPACE TO EXPRESS ANY OTHER IDEAS YOU MAY HAVE ABOUT FACILITIES OR PROVISIONS FOR PETS.* _____

_____

_____

_____

_____

_____

_____

_____

_____

_____

_____

_____

_____

_____

_____

_____

_____

_____

_____

SECTION

2

YOUR NEIGHBORHOOD AND YOUR OWN AREA OF GROUND

Your selection of a place to live is a strong indication of your lifestyle goals. While the decision to live in a given city and state is usually based on an overriding factor such as employment, you often have the opportunity to choose a house or apartment in the city or to live in the suburbs. Condominiums, houseboats, and mobile homes are also possible choices.

If you are planning to live in a house, first consideration should be given to the lot on which the house is, or will be located.

When *buying a home,* the location and character of the lot and the environment of the neighborhood should be just as important to you as the design and construction of the house. The environment and available facilities should suit your lifestyle as well as the house does.

If you are planning to *build a new home* on a building site you now own or are planning to buy, you can — through careful observation — obtain the maximum use of the land, orient the house to the best advantage in relationship to the sun, and design a house that is in harmony with the building site, the surrounding environment, and your own way of life.

If you are *remodeling your own home*, you are well acquainted with your lot. But perhaps you should take a closer look at all of its unique possibilities and advantages and also consider any disadvantages it may have.

When you are *making an addition to a home,* thorough analysis of the lot is particularly necessary and rewarding. In some cases the land seems totally inadequate for the proposed project. However, careful planning often results in ingenious solutions to problem situations.

If your lot situation is settled, answers to the following questions will help in your present planning. If you are making plans for the future, the questions will alert you to some of the many variables to consider before buying or renting property.

PHYSICAL DESCRIPTION OF YOUR LOT

The following questions apply equally to a building site you may now own, or plan to buy, and to a lot with an existing house on it.

1. *LIST THE DIMENSIONS (MEASUREMENTS) OF THE LOT.*

   Width _____ Depth _____

   If your lot is irregular in shape, sketch and dimension it in this space.

2. *IS THE CONTOUR OF THE LOT*

   Flat or easy to level? _____ *Gently sloping?* _____

   Moderate hillside? _____ *Steep hillside?* _____

3. *IS THE LAND MOSTLY*

   Loam? _____ *Adobe?* _____ *Silt?* _____

   Sand? _____ *Gravel?* _____ *Rock?* _____

4. *DESCRIBE ANY ESPECIALLY GOOD FEATURES OF YOUR LOT.* _____

   _____

   _____

5. *IF YOU ARE REMODELING, DESCRIBE ANY OF THE LOT'S FEATURES THAT*
   YOU WOULD LIKE TO TAKE ADVANTAGE OF IN THE NEW DESIGN. _____

   _____

   _____

   _____

6. *DESCRIBE ANY BUILDINGS OR TREES THAT ARE TO REMAIN ON THE LOT.*

   _____

7. IS THE BUILDING SITE CLEARED OF BRUSH, TREES, OLD BUILDINGS, LARGE ROCKS? _____

_____

8. IS THERE ANY SIGN OF EROSION? _____

9. DESCRIBE ANY SPECIAL PROBLEMS THE LOT PRESENTS RELATIVE TO CONSTRUCTION. _____

_____

_____

10. WILL EARTH MOVING BE INVOLVED? _____

_____

11. HAS ANY PART OF THE LAND BEEN FILLED? _____

_____

12. HAS A SOIL COMPACTION TEST BEEN MADE ON YOUR LAND BY A QUALIFIED ENGINEER? _____

13. HAVE YOU CHECKED WITH LOCAL AGENCIES TO DISCOVER ANY IRREGULARITIES IN EARTH FORMATION OR ACTIVITY SUCH AS LAND SLIDE POTENTIAL? _____

14. IF YOUR LOT IS LOCATED IN A WOODED CANYON, HAVE YOU CONSIDERED THE HAZARD OF BRUSH FIRES? _____

15. IS THERE AN ACCESS ROAD TO THE PROPERTY? _____

16. WHAT IMPROVEMENTS HAVE ALREADY BEEN MADE TO THE PROPERTY?

_____

_____

17. DISCUSS ANY PLANS YOU HAVE FOR YOUR LOT. _____

_____

THE DESIGN OF THE HOUSE AS IT RELATES TO THE LOT

Design professionals study the setting and the contour of the land before deciding on the shape and style of the house. If the ground is relatively flat and the lot presents no complexities or unique features, design and style are largely a matter of personal preference — although the house should blend harmoniously with its surroundings.

Maximum use can often be made of a problem building site by designing a home to fit the specific irregularities of that piece of land. For example, a house of more than one level can be planned to fit the contour of a sloping lot. A room, living area, or deck can project beyond the main part of the structure to create even more living space on the steepest side(s) of the lot.

1. *IF YOU ARE PLANNING A NEW HOME OR AN ADDITION, DOES YOUR LAND LEND ITSELF BEST TO*

   A one-story house? _____

   A two-story house? _____

   A split-level house? _____

   Some other kind of structure? _____

2. *WHAT HOUSE SHAPE IS BEST SUITED FOR YOUR LOT?*

   Tall and narrow _____ *Low and rambling* _____

   Oblong _____ *Square* _____

   U shaped _____ *T shaped* _____

   H shaped _____ *L shaped* _____

   Some other shape _____

3. *WHAT KIND OF HOME DESIGN DO YOU REALLY PREFER?*

   _____

   _____

   _____

4. *IF YOU ARE PLANNING TO REMODEL, WHICH OF THE DESIGNS DESCRIBED APPLIES TO YOUR PRESENT HOME?* _____

_____

5. *DO YOU HAVE A SPECIAL ARCHITECTURAL STYLE IN MIND, SUCH AS*

Cape Cod? _____ Spanish or Mediterranean? _____

Contemporary? _____ Contemporary Ranch? _____

Rustic Ranch? _____ Oriental? _____

Salt Box? _____ Other? _____

COMMENTS AND REMINDERS: _____

_____

_____

_____

_____

_____

_____

_____

_____

_____

_____

_____

_____

_____

_____

_____

YOUR LOT HAS ITS OWN SOLAR SYSTEM

Maximum utilization of sun to warm a house in the winter can be achieved by orienting major living areas so that windows face *south*. Rooms with *south*-facing windows will be warmer and easier to heat and they will be flooded with sunlight most of the day during the winter months. Windows will be shaded in the summer, when the angle of the sun is higher, if the house has a fairly wide overhang on the *south* side.

When you have completed your lifestyle profile and made decisions about your space requirements and the way you will use your rooms, you will know which rooms will most often be occupied during daytime hours. For example, kitchens and family rooms are usually occupied in the daytime and would benefit from a *southern* exposure. Your living room might be used more often in the evening; if so, it could face *north*.

Some people enjoy sunlight in the bedrooms in the morning. Early morning sun is available to rooms with windows facing *east*. For late or daytime sleepers bedrooms with windows facing *north* would receive little direct sunlight.

Although rooms facing *north* do not receive direct sunlight, *north* windows do provide excellent working light for projects that require even light throughout the day.

Large windows facing *west* are often undesirable because the summer sun is far too hot in most climates. If you are planning a garage, storage room, or other service-type building, it is advisable to place it on the *west* side to serve as a buffer between the sun and the *west* wall of the house.

Orienting your house to the best advantage is not difficult, and the benefits you gain are many. A little time invested in observing the way the sun casts its rays on your lot can reward you with amazing dividends.

Your answers to the following questions will help you to plan the best utilization of lot space as your house relates to the sun and as you live in your home.

1. IN WHICH ROOMS DO YOU PREFER SUN MOST OF THE DAY? (Southern

exposure) _____

_____

2. IN WHICH ROOMS DO YOU WANT EARLY-MORNING SUN? (Eastern exposure)

_____

_____

_____

3. *IN WHICH ROOMS DO YOU WANT MINIMUM SUN? (Northern exposure)*

_____

_____

4. *WHAT AREA OF THE HOUSE OR GARAGE COULD BE PLACED ON THE WEST SIDE TO SERVE AS A BUFFER TO THE HOT SUMMER SUN?* _____

_____

_____

5. *DISCUSS ANY OTHER IDEAS YOU HAVE RELATIVE TO THE ORIENTATION OF THE HOUSE ON YOUR LOT.* _____

_____

_____

_____

_____

COMMENTS AND REMINDERS: _____

_____

_____

_____

_____

_____

_____

_____

_____

_____

_____

THE CLIMATE OF YOUR AREA AND ITS EFFECT ON YOUR LIFESTYLE

In areas where the climate is mild, it is possible to enjoy outdoor activities most of the year. Homes can be designed to provide maximum facilities for recreation, gardening, and relaxing outdoors.

In locales where weather conditions are extreme, houses must be designed, not only to withstand the elements, but also to provide space for indoor recreation during the long winter months.

Such considerations as the design of the roof, the amount of insulation required, the type and size of the furnace and air-conditioning unit, and the kind of building materials selected, are often directly related to local weather conditions. Study the houses in your area for ideas. You will probably find some good design solutions to weather-related problems.

1. *USE THIS SPACE TO DESCRIBE THE WAYS IN WHICH THE FOLLOWING ELEMENTS AFFECT YOUR LIFESTYLE.*

   Rain, Wind, Snow, Heat, and Humidity _____

   _____

   _____

   _____

   _____

2. *WHAT DESIGN PROVISIONS SHOULD BE MADE, IN YOUR PLANNING, TO MAKE YOUR HOUSE MORE COMFORTABLE WHEN WEATHER CONDITIONS ARE EXTREME?*_____

   _____

   _____

   _____

   _____

   _____

3. WHAT SPECIAL BUILDING MATERIALS HAVE YOU SEEN BEING USED LOCALLY TO COMBAT WEATHER PROBLEMS? _____

_____

_____

4. IF YOU ARE REMODELING, WHAT IMPROVEMENTS WOULD MAKE YOUR HOME MORE COMFORTABLE WHEN WEATHER CONDITIONS ARE EX-TREME?

_____

_____

_____

COMMENTS AND REMINDERS: _____

_____

_____

_____

_____

_____

_____

_____

_____

_____

_____

_____

_____

PRIVACY FROM NEIGHBORS AND STREET

Another important consideration in planning the location of a *new house* on a lot, an *addition* or a *remodeling project* is privacy from neighbors and from the street. Privacy is, in most cases, relatively easy to achieve even when the walls of the house are close to the neighbors' windows or close to the street.

When designing a *new home*, you have the opportunity to arrange windows, entrances, and outdoor living areas for maximum privacy from the start.

When making an *addition to a home* or *remodeling*, strategically placed screens, fencing, shrubs, and trees can serve to transform your home into a private sanctuary. Privacy is not such an important consideration to those individuals who enjoy interaction with their neighbors, but if you are a private person or family, you may wish to give careful thought to the following questions.

1. *IS LACK OF PRIVACY A PROBLEM ON YOUR LOT?* _____

2. *FOR WHAT ROOMS OR AREAS SHOULD YOU MAKE SPECIAL PRIVACY*

   PROVISIONS? _____

   _____

   _____

3. *CAN YOUR PRIVACY FROM NEIGHBORS BE INCREASED BY STRATEGIC*

   PLACEMENT OF

   Fencing? _____

   Screens? _____

   Planting? _____

   Windows? _____

   Drapery at windows? _____

   Other barrier? _____

4. *IF YOU ARE PLANNING A NEW HOME, WILL YOU NEED TO TAKE PRIVACY*

   INTO ACCOUNT? _____

   _____

5. *IN THIS SPACE, DISCUSS ANY PRIVACY PROBLEMS INHERENT IN YOUR LOT SITUATION AND POSSIBLE SOLUTIONS TO THEM.* _____

_____

_____

_____

_____

_____

COMMENTS AND REMINDERS: _____

_____

_____

_____

_____

_____

_____

_____

_____

_____

_____

_____

_____

_____

_____

_____

LOT USE AND LANDSCAPING

When analyzing the use of available lot space and planning the landscaping, your personal lifestyle is again an important consideration.

Answers to the questions that follow will help you to plan the use of lot space as it relates to your neighborhood, weather conditions, privacy, noise pollution, recreational activities, and your personal inclination to maintain a garden.

1. *WHAT PURPOSE SHOULD YOUR LANDSCAPING SERVE?*

   To buffer noise _____

   To block wind _____

   To create shade _____

   To create privacy _____

   To create spaces for recreational activities _____

   To create space for service areas _____

   To satisfy the gardening urge of a family member _____

   To add beauty to the surroundings _____

   To grow food _____

   Any other _____

2. *SHOULD YOU INCLUDE SOME OF THE FOLLOWING LOW-MAINTENANCE*

   FEATURES IN YOUR PLAN?

   Paved, graveled, or rock-covered areas in place of a lawn _____

   Shrubs and trees requiring minimum maintenance _____

   An underground sprinkler system _____

3. *DOES THE GARDENER MEMBER OF THE FAMILY PLAN A MORE AMBITIOUS*

   PROJECT SUCH AS

   A lawn that requires loving care? _____

A vegetable garden? _____

An orchard? _____

Flower beds? _____

Other land use? _____

4. DO YOU PLAN TO UTILIZE THE MAJOR PORTION OF YOUR LOT FOR RECREATIONAL FACILITIES SUCH AS

A swimming pool? _____

A hot tub or spa? _____

A court or space for athletic activities or games? _____

A children's play yard with a gym set and swings? _____

A wading pool? _____

A sand box? _____

Some other facility? _____

5. DO YOU NEED TO ALLOW SPACE FOR PETS? _____

6. DESCRIBE YOUR IDEAS FOR MAKING YOUR LOT SPACE FIT YOUR LIFESTYLE.

_____

_____

_____

COMMENTS AND REMINDERS: _____

_____

_____

_____

_____

_____

SECURITY IN YOUR NEIGHBORHOOD

If you have cause for concern about security in your neighborhood, that apprehension will affect the way you live in your home and in the pleasure you derive from it. Some simple safety measures can be incorporated into your planning that will increase your comfort and security immeasurably.

1. *WILL YOUR HOUSE BE UNOCCUPIED AT TIMES? IF SO, SHOULD YOU CONSIDER:*

    A low-maintenance landscaping plan for the street side — so the house will not look neglected while you are away? _____

    An inconspicuous place where newspapers can be left? _____

    Opaque garage windows so no one can observe the absence of your car? _____

2. *IS YOUR STREET WELL LIGHTED? IF NOT, SHOULD YOU CONSIDER OUT-DOOR LIGHTING THAT TURNS ON AUTOMATICALLY?*

    _____

3. *SHOULD YOU PLAN FOR SECURITY DEVISES SUCH AS*

    Special locks? _____

    Changing locks when you move into a new home? _____

    Key locks for windows and sliding glass doors, where possible? _____

    A burglar alarm system? _____

    An electric, remote-control garage-door opener? _____

    Grills on the windows and at the entrances? _____

    An Intercom system to the front door? _____

    Lights inside the house that turn on automatically? _____

    _____

    _____

4. DISCUSS ANY OTHER SECURITY PROBLEMS RELEVANT TO YOUR SITUATION
AND LIST ANY OTHER SECURITY IDEAS YOU MAY HAVE. _____

_____

_____

_____

_____

_____

_____

COMMENTS AND REMINDERS: _____

_____

_____

_____

_____

_____

_____

_____

_____

_____

_____

_____

_____

_____

AVAILABILITY OF UTILITIES

If you are remodeling your home, water is certainly available to you, either by means of a municipal or private water system or by a pump of your own. But when you are buying land for a new home, the source, location, and cost of obtaining water must be investigated.

You should also verify the availability of electricity and natural gas to your property. Unexpected extra expenses are often incurred when utilities are brought to the lot.

If electricity or natural gas are not available in your location, you will need to investigage alternate energy sources, their availability, and their cost.

The following questions need to be answered to determine your special utility possibilities and requirements.

WATER

1. *IS PUBLIC WATER SERVICE AVAILABLE TO YOUR LOT?* _____

2. *WILL YOU NEED A WELL?* _____

SPACE HEATING

3. *WHICH OF THE FOLLOWING ENERGY SOURCES IS AVAILABLE TO YOUR COMMUNITY IN ADEQUATE SUPPLY?*

   Electricity _____   *Natural gas* _____

   Liquid petroleum gas _____   *Fuel oil* _____

   Coal _____   *Wood* _____

4. *ARE YOU CONSIDERING A SOLAR HEATING SYSTEM?* _____

5. *IF SO, WHAT SOLAR HEATING IDEAS DO YOU HAVE FOR YOUR HOME?* _____

   _____

   _____

   _____

   _____

SEWAGE SYSTEM

6. *IS THERE A PUBLIC SEWAGE SYSTEM AVAILABLE TO YOUR LOT?*

_____

7. *WILL YOU NEED TO INSTALL A SEPTIC SYSTEM?* _____

COMMENTS AND REMINDERS:

_____

_____

_____

_____

_____

_____

_____

_____

_____

_____

_____

_____

_____

_____

_____

_____

_____

ALTERNATE ENERGY SOLUTIONS

If conventional fuel for space or water heating is not readily available to your lot or if you are attempting to conserve your fuel consumption, you may want to investigate the potential of wood- or coal-burning stoves or fireplaces.

Stoves are now available in a variety of sizes and shapes and most are very efficient. Fireplaces can be equipped with devices to increase their efficiency. If fuel such as wood or coal for a stove or fireplace is available to you, it might be wise to consider using one or several for supplementary heat in the winter and to take the chill off the rooms when weather is unseasonably cool. Investigate your local ordinances in regard to wood and/or coal usage.

The potential of solar energy is being developed and many sophisticated — and some not so sophisticated — devices are being designed and manufactured. If you plan to incorporate solar energy into your plan for heating or generating electricity, you are undertaking a real challenge, but some new developments may be worth investigating.

Meantime, there are many simple things you can do to make your home more comfortable and energy-efficient. Some are things anyone can do and the cost is minor compared to the gain in comfort and lowered fuel bills; for example, use of larger windows on the *south* size of your house for greater sun effect in winter and small windows on the *north* side. Double-glazed windows add greatly to the overall efficiency. An attic fan can be installed to discharge summer heat. New homes can be insulated and weather-stripped and insulation can be increased in older homes. Consider incorporating as many passive solar ideas into your plan as possible when you build or remodel. Design goals for everyone should include making the house as energy-efficient as possible.

USE THIS SPACE TO DESCRIBE ANY PLANS YOU HAVE FOR MAKING YOUR

HOUSE MORE ENERGY-EFFICIENT. _____

_____

_____

_____

_____

_____

See SOURCES OF SUPPLEMENTARY INFORMATION in the back of this book for a list of books and publications on passive and active solar systems.

SECTION

3

CREATIVE PLANNING
ROOM BY ROOM

A house is so much more than just a place to live. It can provide room for the growth and fulfillment of potential for each family member. A home that has been designed to meet individual needs will also help to eliminate the annoyances often brought about by inadequate or poorly arranged living spaces.

In SECTION 3, each family member is challenged to undertake serious self-evaluation, examine personal priorities, and express ideas and preferences freely. When you consider all of the divergent personality characteristics, interests, and activities of the persons sharing facilities in a household, it is truly remarkable how well people do adapt to each other and to the home they share! Still, in the interest of harmony, compromises must often be made. When each member of the family has been given the opportunity to make decisions, there will inevitably be some conflict, errors in judgment, and selections that exceed the budget. After everyone has contributed ideas to the plan, careful and critical analysis of the concept as a whole will be necessary.

When this section is completed, a plan will begin to take shape. Your answers to ALTERNATIVES, the last question in each room study, will help you keep the plan flexible and establish alternatives and trade-offs. This will, in the final analysis, simplify the task of making revisions and adjustments when necessary.

As you begin planning individual rooms, you will find it useful to start a file of clippings and ideas for each room. Encourage family members to participate in this activity. Each person can have a file of ideas for his or her own bedroom as well as ideas to contribute for the common living spaces.

Supplement your design concepts by collecting samples and ideas for colors, wall finishes, floor coverings, electrical fixtures, bathroom fixtures, appliances, and furnishings.

YOUR PERSONAL FURNISHINGS CAN FIT THE PLAN

Furniture should be adapted to the existing floor space, but — in long-range planning — it is often possible to utilize many of the pieces you already have in the new plan. If you have accumulated a number of pieces you intend to keep, the style of those pieces might also suggest a style or a decorating theme.

In the next parts of SECTION 3, you will begin to analyze your space requirements in each individual room. It will be useful, as you proceed, to have before you a list of the most important pieces of furniture that you now own — or plan to acquire — for a particular room.

This list should also include the measurements of each piece. Then, when planning progresses to the drawing stage, spaces can, to some extent, be planned to accommodate furnishings or appliances that you now own or intend to acquire. For example, it is particularly important to list bed sizes, such as twin, double, queen or king size, junior, or crib.

The chart on the next page is for your list of each important piece of furniture or any appliances you will be using in the new plan.

1. *WHICH OF THE FOLLOWING STATEMENTS IS APPLICABLE TO YOUR SITUATION?*

   You have not started to acquire furnishings or appliances _____

   You have a few things that you intend to use in the new or remodeled home ____

   You will be adding a few pieces, a little at a time, to what you already have _____

   You have everything you will need to furnish the new or remodeled home _____

2. *DO YOU LIKE TO MIX FURNISHINGS OF DIFFERENT PERIODS AND/OR WOOD FINISHES?* _____

   _____

   _____

   _____

   _____

   _____

3. *DO YOU PLAN TO CARRY OUT ANY DEFINITE STYLE OR THEME SUCH AS*

   Contemporary? _____ *Mediterranean?* _____

   Early American? _____ *Provincial?* _____

   Oriental? _____ *Hawaiian?* _____

   Colonial? _____ *Period?* _____

   Another style or theme? _____

4. *DISCUSS YOUR PLANS FOR FURNISHINGS IN THIS SPACE.* _____

   _____

   _____

   _____

   _____

   _____

   _____

   _____

   _____

   _____

   _____

   _____

   _____

   _____

   _____

   _____

COMMENTS AND REMINDERS: _____

_____

	DESCRIPTION	WIDTH	DEPTH	HEIGHT
ENTRY				
LIVING ROOM				
FAMILY ROOM				
DINING ROOM				
KITCHEN				
LAUNDRY				

	DESCRIPTION	WIDTH	DEPTH	HEIGHT
MASTER BEDROOM				
OTHER ADULT'S BEDROOM				
CHILDREN'S BEDROOM AREA NO. 1				
CHILDREN'S BEDROOM AREA NO. 2				
CHILDREN'S BEDROOM AREA NO. 3 OR NURSERY				
SPECIAL-PURPOSE ROOM				

THE ENTRANCES TO YOUR HOME

The first impression others have of your home is usually experienced at the front door. In some plans the front door opens directly into the main living area. In others, entrance halls are small rooms divided or partially screened from the living areas. A well-planned entry has several functions. One is to welcome guests to the home and to impart a glimpse of your personality and your lifestyle. Another is to screen or shield the rest of the house from the view of strangers arriving at your door. The entry should also serve as a convenient place to remove and hang or store coats, jackets, and rain apparel.

Most homes are designed with a service or rear entrance that serves the kitchen, family room, or service area. For some families, the kitchen and eating area form the focal point for much of the daily activity and social interaction. If this is the case in your family, your service entrance may be the one most often used by friends and neighbors as well as by the family.

The service entrance should provide convenient access to the garage for carrying groceries into the house from the car. It should also provide handy access to the laundry area, workshop, food-storage area and the service area for the garden.

Your answers to the following questions will reflect your own lifestyle and will help you plan the most effective and practical entrances to your home.

1. *WOULD YOU PREFER THE FRONT ENTRANCE TO YOUR HOME TO BE*

   Completely separated from other living areas? _____

   Partially screened from other living areas? _____

   Another arrangement? _____

2. *WHICH ENTRANCE WILL THE FAMILY USE MOST OFTEN?*

   Front or main _____ *Service or rear* _____

   Garage _____ *Other* _____

3. *WHICH ENTRANCE WILL BE USED BY MOST OF YOUR GUESTS?*

   Front or main _____ *Service or rear* _____

   Garage _____ *Other* _____

   _____

   _____

4. SO THAT YOU CAN SEE THE PERSON AT THE FRONT DOOR BEFORE OPEN-
ING IT, WHICH OF THE FOLLOWING ARRANGEMENTS WOULD YOU
PREFER?

A window to provide a view of the front entrance _____

Glass panel(s) in the door _____

A peephole viewer built into the door _____

A wall or door panel of one-way glass _____

5. WHAT SPECIAL STORAGE REQUIREMENTS WILL YOU HAVE FOR THE MAIN
ENTRANCE? _____

6. WHAT ITEMS SHOULD LOGICALLY BE STORED NEAR THE BACK OR SERVICE
ENTRANCE? _____

7. WHAT IDEAS OR REQUIREMENTS UNIQUE TO YOUR OWN LIFESTYLE DO
YOU HAVE FOR EITHER ENTRANCE? _____

8. LIST ELECTRICAL OUTLETS REQUIRED IN THE ENTRY FOR SPECIAL ITEMS
SUCH AS CLOCKS OR LAMPS. _____

9. WHAT ARE YOUR PLANS FOR GENERAL ROOM ILLUMINATION? _____

_____

10. SHOULD YOU BE ABLE TO SWITCH ON OUTDOOR LIGHTING FROM THE
FRONT OR BACK ENTRANCE? _____

11. LIST ANY SPECIAL ELECTRICAL REQUIREMENTS YOU MAY HAVE FOR THIS
AREA. _____

_____

_____

_____

_____

12. LIST ANY TENTATIVE IDEAS YOU HAVE FOR COLOR AND DECORATIVE TREATMENT OF THE ENTRANCE. _____

_____

_____

_____

13. WOULD YOU LIKE TO USE A HARD-SURFACED, EASILY CLEANED FLOOR COVERING IN YOUR ENTRY AREA SUCH AS LINOLEUM OR CERAMIC TILE? DESCRIBE YOUR FLOOR COVERING IDEAS IN THIS SPACE.

_____

_____

_____

ALTERNATIVES:

If, in the final analysis, the budget must be cut, what alternatives would be acceptable to you in this area?

_____

_____

_____

COMMENTS AND REMINDERS: _____

_____

_____

_____

_____

_____

_____

YOUR LIVING-ROOM PLANS

To plan the ideal living room for your lifestyle, you must spend some time analyzing the way you use your present living room and visualizing optimum facilities to accommodate whatever activities might take place in the living room of your future home.

In small homes, the living room is truly a multipurpose room. If the house is to be larger, some living-room functions might take place in rooms especially planned for them, e.g., a recreation room for watching television, a separate dining room, or a library for housing books and reading.

. It is therefore necessary to make an overall living-room plan based on the way you live and on the functions of the room. Answers to the questions that follow will guide you in assessing your priorities and in planning living-room space in accordance with your personal requirements.

1. WILL YOUR FAMILY USE THE LIVING ROOM AS

A family gathering place for interaction:

between adults? _____

between adults and children? _____

A quiet retreat for adults? _____

A special-occasion room? _____

2. FOR WHAT KIND OF ENTERTAINING WILL YOU USE THE LIVING ROOM?

Formal and/or informal adult gatherings _____

Children entertaining their friends _____

Adults' club or business meetings _____

Children's club meetings _____

3. WHAT ACTIVITIES WILL TAKE PLACE IN THE LIVING ROOM?

Adults and/or children playing cards or other quiet games _____

Watching television _____

Playing a piano or other musical instrument(s) _____

Listening to recorded music _____

Reading _____

Showing home slides or movies _____

Studying by adults and/or children _____

Working at a desk (home office) _____

Dining or serving drinks and snacks _____

4. WILL YOU REQUIRE SPACE OR STORAGE FACILITIES FOR ANY OF THE
   FOLLOWING?

Stereo components _____ Records and/or tapes _____

Photo equipment _____ Television _____

Game table _____ Desk or study table _____

Bookshelves _____

Special seating arrangements _____

Provisions for serving food and/or beverages _____

Piano or other musical instrument(s) _____

Collections _____

Other _____

5. IS THE LIVING ROOM A SPACE WHERE YOU WOULD LIKE TO HAVE LARGE
   PICTURE WINDOWS? (Consider orientation of the house to the sun.) _____

6. WILL YOU WANT A PATIO DOOR TO PROVIDE ACCESS TO A TERRACE,
   PATIO, OR DECK? _____

7. LIST LAMPS AND SPECIAL EQUIPMENT FOR WHICH YOU WILL NEED
   ELECTRICAL OUTLETS IN THE LIVING ROOM. _____

   _____

8. WHAT IDEAS DO YOU HAVE FOR

General room illumination? _____

Special accent lighting? _____

Other lighting? _____

9. WILL YOU NEED A RECEPTACLE FOR A TELEVISION ANTENNA OR CABLE IN

THE LIVING ROOM? _____

10. DO YOU PLAN TO HAVE A TELEPHONE IN THE LIVING ROOM? _____

11. LIST ANY TENTATIVE IDEAS YOU HAVE FOR COLOR AND DECORATIVE

TREATMENT OF THE LIVING ROOM. _____

_____

_____

_____

12. DESCRIBE ANY FLOOR-COVERING IDEAS YOU MAY HAVE FOR THE LIVING

ROOM.

_____

_____

_____

_____

_____

13. DESCRIBE ANY IDEAS YOU HAVE THAT ARE UNIQUE TO YOUR LIFESTYLE.

_____

_____

_____

_____

_____

ALTERNATIVES:

If, in the final analysis, the budget must be cut, what alternatives would be acceptable to you for the living room?

_____

_____

_____

COMMENTS AND REMINDERS: _____

_____

_____

_____

_____

_____

_____

_____

_____

_____

_____

_____

_____

_____

_____

_____

PLANNING FOR FIREPLACES AND STOVES

An open, wood-burning masonry fireplace adds beauty, warmth, and cheer to a room and is an important feature in many homes. However, national awareness of fuel shortages, air pollution, and the necessity for energy conservation have caused many people to reevaluate the efficiency of wood-burning fireplaces in comparison with various types of wood-burning stoves. If maximum utilization of wood or coal for heating your home is the primary consideration, an airtight stove or furnace is ranked first in efficiency. Unfortunately, this type of stove or furnace lacks the attractiveness of the open fire.

The Franklin-type stove is designed with iron doors in the front that can be opened so that you can see the fire burning. The doors can also be closed to create airtight efficiency. Some models of the Franklin-type stove have transparent panels in the doors, permitting a view of the fire when the doors are closed.

If your first choice is a fireplace and you plan to use a gas, oil, electric, or coal furnace for primary heating, there are several things that can be done to increase fireplace efficiency and to prevent the heated air in the room from escaping up the chimney. One is to install glass doors, tightly fitted, over the firebox opening. These fit the opening in the same way as the more commonly used recessed firescreens. Another is to include an air-circulating (convection) system which draws air from the room through the bottom of the firebox, channels it around the firebox and discharges it, fully heated, back into the room. Some types of units can be installed most easily while the fireplace is under construction. Similar units are also available for installation in existing fireplaces.

Another possible choice is a fireplace constructed of metal. This type is available in a choice of built-in models as well as in attractive free-standing designs that can be installed in almost any location in the room.

Prefabricated metal fireplaces of all types are becoming increasingly popular because most of them are slightly more efficient than the masonry types and they are easy to install and lightweight. These factors make them particularly desirable for second-floor installation.

Many of these prefabricated units are available with built-in, air-circulating systems. Moreover, when built-in prefabricated fireplaces are installed, they can be faced with any of the standard masonry, tile, or panel treatments used on masonry fireplaces.

The decision you make must be based on your own lifestyle. If you enjoy an open fire and have access to wood as well as to other types of fuels for your primary heating source, you will probably want a fireplace. If wood or coal is available to you in abundance, and if it is your most reliable source of fuel, the more efficient types of stoves are your best choice.

Consider the following questions when deciding whether to include a stove or a fireplace in your plans.

FIREPLACES

1. *WOULD YOUR FIREPLACE BE USED*

   For special occasions only? _____

   Often, for supplementary heat? _____

2. *WHICH TYPE OF FIREPLACE WOULD BEST SUIT YOUR PURPOSE?*

   Masonry _____

   Prefabricated metal:

       Built-in _____

       Free-standing _____

3. *DO YOU PLAN TO EQUIP YOUR FIREPLACE WITH*

   An air-circulating system? _____

   Glass doors in place of a firescreen? _____

   Other accessories? _____

4. *WHERE WOULD YOU LIKE TO HAVE A FIREPLACE?*

   Living room _____ *Kitchen* _____

   Family room _____ *Master bedroom* _____

   Dining room _____ *Special-purpose room* _____

   Other location(s) _____

   _____

5. *WHICH OF THE FOLLOWING BUILT-IN FIREPLACE SHAPES BEST FIT(S) YOUR*

   PLANS?

   Open front, conventional (most efficient) _____

   Open front, corner (most efficient) _____

   Open front and one side, corner (not as efficient) _____

   Open front and back, see-through facing two rooms (not as efficient) _____

Two open-front fireplaces constructed back to back (most efficient) _____

Other design type(s) _____

6. A MASONRY OR METAL FIREPLACE COULD BE SURFACED WITH ANY OF THE FOLLOWING MATERIALS. WHICH WOULD YOU PREFER?

Brick _____ *Stone* _____ *Other masonry* _____

Tile _____ *Terrazzo* _____ *Stucco* _____

Paneling _____ *Gypsum board* _____ *Other facing material* _____

7. IF YOU ARE REMODELING,

Do you have a fireplace to work with? _____

What are your plans for it? _____

_____

_____

In what room is it located? _____

8. DO YOU PLAN TO ADD A FIREPLACE WHEN YOU REMODEL? _____

9. DESCRIBE YOUR PLANS HERE. _____

_____

_____

10. DO YOU PLAN TO INSTALL

A log lighter? _____ *An ash clean-out?* _____

11. WHAT OTHER FIREPLACE IDEAS DO YOU HAVE? _____

_____

_____

_____

_____

STOVES

12. *DO YOUR PLANS CALL FOR THE USE OF ONE OR MORE STOVES?* _____

13. *IF SO, WHAT AREAS OF THE HOUSE WOULD BE HEATED WITH STOVES?* ____

_____

14. *WHICH OF THE FOLLOWING TYPES OF STOVES DO YOU PLAN TO USE?*

An airtight stove _____

A Franklin-type stove _____

An airtight, wood-burning furnace _____

A wood-burning furnace with circulating fan and thermostat _____

A wood-burning furnace with a supplementary gas or oil burner as a part of the

system _____

Other type _____

15. *DO YOU EXPECT TO NEED HEAT FROM ANOTHER SOURCE TO SUPPLEMENT*

YOUR WOOD-BURNING STOVE? _____

_____

16. *HAVE YOU CONSIDERED A WOOD-BURNING COOKSTOVE IN THE KITCHEN*

FOR SUPPLEMENTARY OR EMERGENCY USE? _____

17. *DO YOU PLAN TO COOK ON A WOOD-BURNING STOVE FULL-TIME?* _____

18. *COULD YOU UTILIZE THE CHIMNEY OF AN EXISTING FIREPLACE FOR A*

NEW WOOD-BURNING STOVE? _____

19. *WHAT SPECIAL IDEAS DO YOU HAVE THAT ARE RELEVANT TO HEATING*

YOUR HOUSE WITH WOOD? _____

_____

20. *WHAT SPECIAL IDEAS DO YOU HAVE FOR USING STOVES?* _____

_____

IS A FAMILY ROOM FOR YOU?

Your lifestyle and the way you live in a home will really determine your need for space for family activities. If you wish to reserve your living room for entertaining guests or as a quiet and tidy retreat for adults, you may want a family room. Family rooms are usually flexible spaces designed to have several functions. They can provide space for dining or snacking, watching television, playing, or working on projects.

The family room is probably the most versatile living space in the house and is often the setting for social interaction between family members. In some plans, it is a space adjacent to or combined with the kitchen. In other plans, the family room flows together with the living room and can be used as an extension of that area when desirable. Another interpretation of the family room might be a recreation room located in another area of the house — away from the kitchen or living room.

If provisions have been made for typical family-room functions in other parts of the house, a family room may not be necessary. Far too many family rooms become a kind of catchall for miscellaneous activities not provided for in any other place in the house.

Your answers to the following questions will help you to analyze the ways in which you might use a family room and whether or not it would be suitable for your family.

1. IF A SEPARATE FAMILY ROOM IS DESIRED, DO YOU PREFER

A room that is open to or close to the kitchen but separate from it? _____

A room that is located in another part of the house? _____

2. WHAT ACTIVITIES WILL PROBABLY TAKE PLACE IN THE FAMILY ROOM?

Eating _____ *Reading or studying* _____

Watching television _____ *Listening to music* _____

Watching home movies _____ *Sewing or other projects* _____

Playing cards or games by adults or children _____

Playing with toys by small children _____

Washing, folding, and/or ironing clothes _____

Other activities _____

_____

3. WILL YOU NEED STORAGE OR FLOOR SPACE FOR

Stereo components, records, and/or tapes? _____

Photo equipment? _____ Books? _____

Television? _____ Card tables? _____

Games and/or toys? _____ Collections? _____

Hobby or sports equipment? _____

Piano and/or other musical instrument(s) and music books and racks? _____

Sewing materials and equipment? _____

Cages, tanks, or beds for pets? _____

4. WHAT SPECIAL SEATING ARRANGEMENTS ARE REQUIRED? _____

_____

5. DO YOU WANT ANY BUILT-INS SUCH AS FOLD-DOWN TABLES FOR A

SEWING MACHINE, GAMES, OR PROJECTS? _____

_____

6. LIST ANY OTHER SPECIAL SPACE ARRANGEMENTS OR STORAGE

REQUIREMENTS YOU MAY HAVE FOR THE FAMILY ROOM. _____

_____

_____

_____

_____

7. IS THE FAMILY ROOM A PLACE WHERE YOU WOULD LIKE TO HAVE LARGE

PICTURE WINDOWS? (Consider orientation to the sun) _____

8. WILL YOU WANT A PATIO DOOR TO PROVIDE ACCESS TO A TERRACE,

PATIO, OR DECK? _____

9. LIST LAMPS AND SPECIAL EQUIPMENT FOR WHICH YOU WILL NEED ELECTRICAL OUTLETS IN THE FAMILY ROOM. _____

_____

_____

10. WHAT IDEAS DO YOU HAVE FOR

General room illumination? _____

Special accent lighting? _____

Other forms of lighting? _____

11. WILL YOU NEED A RECEPTACLE FOR A TELEVISION ANTENNA OR CABLE IN THE FAMILY ROOM? _____

12. DO YOU PLAN TO HAVE A TELEPHONE IN THE FAMILY ROOM? _____

13. LIST ANY TENTATIVE IDEAS YOU HAVE FOR COLOR AND DECORATIVE TREATMENT OF THIS ROOM. _____

_____

_____

_____

14. DESCRIBE ANY FLOOR COVERING IDEAS YOU MAY HAVE FOR THE FAMILY ROOM. _____

_____

_____

15. LIST IDEAS UNIQUE TO YOUR LIFESTYLE AS THEY APPLY TO THE FAMILY ROOM. _____

_____

_____

_____

ALTERNATIVES:

If, in the final analysis, the budget must be cut, what alternatives would be acceptable to you?

_____

_____

_____

_____

COMMENTS AND REMINDERS:

When the laundry room is located in or near the family room, you should consider some of the following disadvantages:

- Noise and heat from laundry appliances
- Odor from laundry products and bleaches

_____

_____

_____

_____

_____

_____

_____

_____

_____

_____

_____

_____

YOUR KITCHEN AND DINING AREA

Efficient design is usually the main goal of kitchen planning, but each person has a different idea about the use of space and the arrangement of facilities. Individual habits, attitudes about food preparation and kitchen work, and the number of people who will be preparing food in the kitchen are all important considerations when kitchens are being planned.

For some, the kitchen is the hub of family activity and an adequate family-sized kitchen is a must. When several family members cook, and perhaps children or guests help, the kitchen, combined with a family or dining area, is often the center of family life. This space is sometimes the warmest, most lived-in area of the house — an area offering ample opportunity for social interaction as well as convenient facilities for food preparation, serving, and dining.

Other people prefer small efficiency kitchens. This is particularly true where one person prepares most of the meals and does the clean-up chores without help. Often, the objective here is to complete kitchen work and be out of the kitchen in the shortest possible time. In this case, the kitchen should be designed and equipped to suit the work habits of that one person.

In another situation, meal preparation may be enjoyed and shared, but a separate dining room or family room may be preferred for dining and social interaction. Plans for dining and serving should logically be an integral part of kitchen planning.

Because the kitchen will probably be the most expensive space in the home — and the space where some family member(s) will be spending a lot of time, it warrants very careful planning. It takes time, thought, and research to plan a kitchen that truly serves your needs and fits your lifestyle.

Answers to the following questions will help you to analyze your own specific requirements.

YOUR WORK HABITS

1. *WHICH FAMILY MEMBER USUALLY SPENDS THE MOST TIME IN THE KITCHEN?* _____

2. *DOES ANYONE USUALLY WORK ALONE IN THE KITCHEN?* _____

3. *WILL THERE BE TIMES WHEN GUESTS HELP IN THE KITCHEN?* _____

4. *DO SMALL CHILDREN WANT TO HELP?* _____

_____

5. IS THERE A GOURMET COOK IN THE FAMILY WHO OFTEN COOKS FROM SCRATCH, BAKES BREAD OR PASTRIES, AND CANS, DRIES, OR FREEZES FOOD? _____

6. TO SAVE TIME, DOES YOUR FAMILY USE A GREAT MANY (COMMERCIALLY) CANNED, FROZEN, OR PREPARED FOODS? _____

THE SIZE OF YOUR REGULAR MEALS

7. HOW MANY PEOPLE ARE AT HOME

For breakfast? _____ For lunch? _____

For dinner? _____

8. DO CHILDREN TAKE THEIR LUNCHES TO SCHOOL? _____

9. DO ADULTS TAKE THEIR LUNCHES TO WORK? _____

10. HOW MANY TAKEOUT LUNCHES MUST BE PREPARED? _____

ENTERTAINING

11. HOW MANY PEOPLE DO YOU EXPECT TO ENTERTAIN AT ONE TIME?

For a sit-down meal _____ For a buffet _____

For luncheons _____ For beverages _____

For adult and/or children's club or business meetings _____

For dessert _____

On the spur of the moment:

Adults _____ Children _____

SERVING MEALS

BREAKFAST

12. HOW MANY FAMILY MEMBERS SIT DOWN TO A COMPLETE BREAKFAST? _____

13. DOES EVERYONE EAT AT THE SAME TIME, OR DOES EACH PERSON EAT AT A TIME TO FIT HIS/HER OWN TIME SCHEDULE? _____

14. DOES ONE PERSON COOK EVERYONE'S BREAKFAST, OR DO SOME PREPARE THEIR OWN? _____

LUNCH

15. ARE SEVERAL PEOPLE HOME FOR LUNCH AND IS A SIT-DOWN MEAL SERVED? _____

16. DOES ONE PERSON PREPARE LUNCH, OR DOES EACH FIX HIS/HER OWN?

_____

17. ARE THERE OFTEN GUESTS FOR LUNCH? _____

DINNER

18. DOES ONE PERSON USUALLY SERVE FAMILY MEALS, OR DO OTHERS HELP?

_____

19. WHEN THERE ARE GUESTS, WHO SERVES THE MEALS? _____

DINING ARRANGEMENT PREFERENCES

BREAKFAST

20. WOULD YOU PREFER TO SERVE BREAKFAST

In the kitchen? _____ In the family room? _____

At a counter or breakfast bar in the kitchen or family room? _____

In a separate breakfast or dining room? _____

On a tray in the bedroom? _____ In another place? _____

LUNCH

21. WHERE WOULD YOU PREFER TO SERVE LUNCH

For the family? _____

For guests? _____

DINNER

22. FOR SERVING FAMILY DINNERS, WHICH ARRANGEMENT WOULD YOU PREFER?

A formal or completely separate dining room _____

An informal space open to the living room _____

A table in the family room _____

A kitchen table _____

23. WHEN SERVING GUESTS, WHICH ARRANGEMENT WOULD YOU PREFER?

A formal or completely separate dining room _____

An informal space, open to the living room _____

A table in the family room _____ A kitchen table _____

DINING AND TELEVISION

24. DO ADULTS AND/OR CHILDREN EAT MEALS WHILE VIEWING TELEVISION?

_____

25. AT WHICH MEALS DOES THIS USUALLY OCCUR? _____

26. DESCRIBE SPECIAL SERVING AND DINING ARRANGEMENTS NEEDED FOR THIS. _____

_____

OUTDOOR DINING FACILITIES

27. IF YOU LIVE IN AN AREA WHERE THE WEATHER IS CONDUCIVE TO OUTDOOR LIVING AND YOU ENJOY EATING OUTDOORS, WHAT FACILITIES ARE NEEDED?

A serving counter _____

A serving bar (pass-through from the kitchen) _____

A table and chairs or benches _____

A barbecue:

Wood- or charcoal-burning _____ *Electric* _____ *Gas* _____

SERVING BEVERAGES

28. DO YOU NEED A SPECIAL PLACE FOR PREPARING AND SERVING HOT OR COLD BEVERAGES? _____ IF SO, WHERE SHOULD IT BE LOCATED?

_____

29. SHOULD IT BE EQUIPPED WITH

A small sink? _____ *A counter for preparing and serving?* _____

A cupboard for storing cups, glasses, beverages, etc.? _____

FOOD PREPARATION

FACILITIES

30. DO YOU NEED SPECIAL PREPARATION SPACE FOR ANY OF THESE?

Baking foods _____ *Canning* _____

Drying _____ *Smoking foods* _____

Freezing foods _____ *Other projects* _____

APPLIANCES

31. THE FOLLOWING ARE SOME OF THE TYPES OF STOVES AND OVENS AVAILABLE. WHICH TYPE DO YOU PREFER?

A combination range with cooktop and oven below or above _____

A combination range with cooktop and two ovens, one below and one above ____

A combination range with two ovens below the cooktop _____

A separate cooktop and a wall oven _____

32. SHOULD THE COOKTOP HAVE TWO, FOUR, OR SIX BURNERS OR FOUR BURNERS AND A GRILL OR BARBECUE? _____

_____

33. DO YOU PREFER

Electric coil burners? _____ Gas burners? _____

An electric, ceramic cooktop? _____

34. DO YOU PLAN TO HAVE A SINGLE OR DOUBLE OVEN? _____

35. SHOULD IT BE

Continuous cleaning? _____ Self-cleaning? _____ Standard? _____

36. DO YOU PLAN TO USE

Gas appliances? _____ Electric appliances? _____ A combination of both? _____

37. WILL YOU BE COOKING ON A WOOD STOVE

Occasionally? _____ Full time? _____

38. DO YOU HAVE, OR PLAN TO BUY, A MICROWAVE OVEN? _____

39. SHOULD IT BE LOCATED

On a counter? _____ In a wall cabinet? _____ In another location? _____

40. DO YOU PLAN TO USE A BARBECUE INDOORS? _____

41. WILL IT BE A BUILT-IN, VENTED APPLIANCE? _____

42. WILL IT OPERATE ON GAS OR ELECTRICALLY HEATED CERAMIC

BRIQUETTES? _____

43. IS A MASONRY FIREPLACE-TYPE BARBECUE PREFERRED? _____

PLUMBING FIXTURES

44. WHICH OF THE FOLLOWING SINK CHOICES WOULD BEST SUIT YOUR

NEEDS?

A shallow single sink _____ A deep single sink _____

A double sink with one side deep and one side shallow _____

A double sink with both sides deep _____

Two deep sinks with a third, smaller, shallow sink in the center for the garbage-

disposal unit _____

FOOD STORAGE
FACILITIES

45. DO YOU HAVE A LOCATION IN MIND, OTHER THAN THE KITCHEN, FOR STORAGE OF EITHER PERISHABLE OR NONPERISHABLE FOODS? _____

46. COULD YOU INSTALL A FREEZER OR STORE NON-PERISHABLE FOODS IN

A basement? _____ A storeroom? _____ A garage? _____

Another location? _____

APPLIANCES

47. WHICH OF THE FOLLOWING APPLIANCES WILL SERVE YOUR STORAGE NEEDS FOR PERISHABLE FOODS?

A refrigerator with a freezer section _____

A separate refrigerator plus a chest- or upright-type freezer _____

STORAGE

48. WHAT KITCHEN STORAGE SPACE WILL BE NEEDED FOR OTHER TYPES OF FOOD?

A large, walk-in pantry _____

Open shelves, floor to ceiling _____

Closed cabinets, floor to ceiling _____

CABINETS

49. WHAT TYPE OF CABINETS DO YOU PREFER FOR FOOD STORAGE? _____

_____

50. DO YOU HAVE THINGS OF AN UNUSUAL SIZE TO STORE SUCH AS

Extra-large cooking utensils? _____

A great many small appliances or kitchen gadgets? _____

Lots of china, glassware, and flatware? _____

Other items? _____

51. DO YOU PREFER HAVING SMALL APPLIANCES AND DRY FOODSTUFFS OUT, ON TOP OF COUNTERS, OR DO YOU KEEP EVERYTHING PUT AWAY IN CABINETS, ON SHELVES, OR IN DRAWERS? _____

_____

52. WHAT TYPE OF STORAGE SPACE DO YOU PREFER FOR CLEANING SUPPLIES AND EQUIPMENT? _____

53. DESCRIBE SPECIAL STORAGE SPACE YOU WILL NEED FOR OTHER ITEMS.

_____

_____

54. DESCRIBE THE TYPE OF CABINETS YOU HAVE IN MIND FOR GENERAL STORAGE. _____

_____

_____

_____

CLEAN-UP

APPLIANCES

55. WHAT APPLIANCES WILL BE NEEDED AT CLEAN-UP TIME?

A dishwasher, either portable or built-in _____

A trash compactor _____

A garbage-disposal unit _____

Installed in the right- _____or left-hand sink _____ or in the center _____

56. WHO USUALLY CLEANS UP AFTER FOOD IS PREPARED? _____

57. WHO USUALLY CLEANS UP AFTER FOOD IS SERVED?

One person _____ Several people _____

_____

58. *WHAT SPECIAL FACILITIES WOULD YOU LIKE TO INCORPORATE IN YOUR PLAN TO MAKE CLEAN-UP TIME EASIER AND MORE PLEASANT?* _____

_____

OTHER FACILITIES

59. *WHAT SPECIAL ITEMS DO YOU WANT IN OR NEAR THE KITCHEN?*

A telephone _____ *A radio* _____ *A television* _____

A desk for meal planning and telephoning _____

Shelves for cookbooks _____

Other ideas _____

_____

DINING ARRANGEMENTS

60. *DO YOU NEED A SEPARATE DINING ROOM?* _____

61. *WOULD AN AREA OF THE LIVING ROOM SERVE AS WELL?* _____

62. *WILL MOST MEALS BE SERVED IN THE KITCHEN? IF SO, WHAT SPECIAL ARRANGEMENT DO YOU PREFER?*

A serving bar _____ *A table* _____ *Both* _____

63. *ARE YOU CONSIDERING A SEPARATE BREAKFAST ROOM?* _____

64. *WILL MEALS EVER BE SERVED IN THE FAMILY ROOM?* _____

65. *IN WHAT OTHER PLACES MIGHT PEOPLE EAT MEALS?* _____

66. *WILL YOU NEED STORAGE FACILITIES NEAR YOUR PRIMARY DINING AREA FOR*

Table leaves? _____ *Large serving pieces?* _____

Extra chairs? _____ *Card tables?* _____

Table linen? _____ *Silver?* _____ *Other equipment?* _____

_____

67. WHAT SIZE AND TYPE OF WINDOWS DO YOU PREFER FOR THE KITCHEN AND FOR THE DINING AREA? _____

_____

_____

ELECTRICAL REQUIREMENTS

68. WHAT ARE YOUR PLANS FOR GENERAL ROOM ILLUMINATION IN THE KITCHEN?

Central fixture(s) _____ Recessed fluorescent ceiling lights _____

Other ideas _____

69. LIST YOUR IDEAS FOR SPOTLIGHTING WORK AREAS. _____

_____

70. WHAT ARE YOUR PLANS FOR GENERAL ROOM ILLUMINATION FOR THE DINING ROOM? _____

_____

71. LIST ELECTRICAL OUTLETS REQUIRED IN THE KITCHEN FOR SPECIAL ITEMS.

110-volt for small appliances _____ 110-volt refrigerator and/or freezer _____

220-volt for an electric range and an oven _____

72. LIST ANY SPECIAL ELECTRICAL OUTLET REQUIREMENTS IN THE DINING ROOM OR DINING AREA.

_____

_____

73. LIST ANY REQUIREMENTS RELEVANT TO LIGHT SWITCHES FOR THE KITCHEN AND FOR THE DINING ROOM OR DINING AREA. _____

_____

COLOR, FINISHES, AND DECORATIVE TREATMENT

74. LIST ANY TENTATIVE IDEAS YOU HAVE FOR COLOR AND DECORATIVE TREATMENT OF THE KITCHEN AND OF THE DINING ROOM OR DINING AREA. _____

_____

_____

_____

75. WHAT TYPE OF COUNTER-TOP SURFACING MATERIAL DO YOU PREFER? Ceramic tile _____ Plastic laminate (known under several brand names such as Formica) _____ Another type _____

76. WHAT OTHER IDEAS DO YOU HAVE ABOUT THE SIZE, ARRANGEMENT, AND LOCATION OF COUNTER TOPS? _____

_____

_____

_____

77. WHAT IDEAS DO YOU HAVE FOR FLOOR COVERING FOR THE KITCHEN AND FOR THE DINING AREA? _____

_____

78. LIST ANY SPECIAL IDEAS UNIQUE TO YOUR LIFESTYLE WHICH APPLY TO THE KITCHEN. _____

_____

_____

79. LIST ANY SPECIAL IDEAS UNIQUE TO YOUR LIFESTYLE WHICH APPLY TO THE DINING FACILITIES. _____

_____

ALTERNATIVES:

If, in the final analysis, the budget must be cut, what alternatives would be acceptable to you ?

_____

_____

COMMENTS AND REMINDERS: _____

A CONVENIENT LAUNDRY AREA

A compact, efficient laundry center can be located anywhere in the house that is convenient for you. Stereotyped ideas about washing and drying clothes are giving way to more realistic and personalized approaches to the matter of handling the family laundry.

Washing machines and dryers are compactly designed for installation in any convenient location in the house where there is access to hot and cold water and a place to install a vent for the dryer.

You can easily determine the most suitable location for your laundry center by analyzing the way you will live and work in your home. If, for example, the person doing the laundry will simultaneously be cooking while also keeping an eye on small children, the laundry center should be in or near the kitchen or family room.

Because most of the laundry accumulates in the bedroom area, some people prefer a laundry center in a space adjacent to the bedrooms. This location is also convenient for putting away clean clothing and linen.

Garages or basements are often used for laundry appliances, but more convenient solutions can usually be found. A well-located separate utility room is ideal, when space permits, and it can be designed to serve several purposes. A sewing center can often share space with a laundry center. A utility room might double as a service entrance, a plant-care room, and a place to remove and hang rain clothing as well as wash off mud. Consider each possible location before making a final decision.

1. WHICH FAMILY MEMBER(S) WILL MOST OFTEN BE DOING THE

   LAUNDRY? _____

2. IS LAUNDRY USUALLY DONE

   In the morning? _____ In the afternoon? _____ In the evening? _____

3. WOULD NOISE FROM THE LAUNDRY EQUIPMENT OCCUR AT SUCH HOURS

   THAT IT WOULD DISTURB OTHER FAMILY MEMBERS? _____

4. TO WHAT AREA OF THE HOUSE SHOULD THE LAUNDRY CENTER BE

   CONVENIENT?

   The kitchen _____ The family room _____

   Upstairs bedrooms _____ Downstairs bedrooms _____

   A nursery _____ The service entrance _____

5. *SHOULD THE LAUNDRY CENTER BE LOCATED*

   In the kitchen or family room? _____

   In a cabinet near the bedroom area? _____

   In a separate utility room? _____

   In a compartmentalized bathroom? _____

   In a garage? _____

   In a basement? _____

   Elsewhere? _____

   _____

6. *IF YOUR PLANS ARE FOR A TWO-STORY HOUSE, WILL YOU NEED A LAUNDRY CHUTE?* _____

7. *IF YOUR CHOICE IS A SEPARATE LAUNDRY ROOM, WHAT OTHER ACTIVITIES MIGHT TAKE PLACE IN THE SAME SPACE?*

   Ironing, hanging clothes, folding clothes _____

   Sewing and/or mending _____

   Projects of family members _____

   Feeding pets _____

   Caring for house plants _____

   Other activities _____

8. *WHAT TYPE OF WASHING MACHINE AND CLOTHES DRYER WOULD BEST FIT THE SPACE YOU HAVE CHOSEN?*

   Side-by-side units _____

   Built-in units installed under the counter (front-loading) _____

   Units stacked, one on top of the other _____

   Small portable units _____

9. WHAT OTHER FACILITIES WILL YOU NEED IN THE LAUNDRY AREA?

A laundry sink _____

Cabinets for storing laundry supplies _____

Space to fold clothes and linen _____

Space to hang clothing _____

Other facilities _____

10. WHERE DO YOU PREFER TO IRON?

In the family room _____

In the laundry center _____

In the kitchen _____

In another location _____

11. WOULD A BUILT-IN IRONING BOARD BE USEFUL IN ONE OF THE ABOVE

LOCATIONS? _____

12. FOR WHICH OF THE FOLLOWING ITEMS WILL YOU NEED CABINETS OR

STORAGE SPACE?

An iron and a portable ironing board _____

A hamper for sorting and storing laundry _____

Items to be ironed _____

13. WHAT SPECIAL STORAGE AND CABINETRY REQUIREMENTS DO YOU HAVE

FOR YOUR LAUNDRY CENTER? _____

_____

14. LIST SPECIAL ELECTRICAL OUTLETS REQUIRED FOR LAUNDRY-CENTER

APPLIANCES AND EQUIPMENT.

110-volt outlet for a washing machine _____ 220-volt outlet for a dryer _____

110-volt outlet for an iron _____ Other _____

15. WHAT ARE YOUR PLANS FOR GENERAL ILLUMINATION OF THE LAUNDRY

AREA? _____

_____

_____

16. LIST ANY TENTATIVE IDEAS YOU HAVE ABOUT COLOR AND DECORATIVE

TREATMENT OF THE LAUNDRY ROOM OR AREA. _____

_____

17. WHAT IDEAS DO YOU HAVE FOR FLOOR COVERING FOR THIS SPACE? ____

_____

ALTERNATIVES:

If, in the final analysis, the budget must be cut, what alternatives would be acceptable to you for this room?

_____

_____

COMMENTS AND REMINDERS:

Locate clothes dryers near an outside wall if possible for ease of venting.

Base your choice of gas or electrical laundry equipment upon the availability and cost of gas and electricity in your community.

Select a location for the laundry that is near other plumbing in the plan or existing house.

Allow enough extra space around equipment to move it in and out for servicing.

_____

_____

_____

_____

_____

EFFICIENT BATHROOMS

To plan an efficient bathroom, one must consider each individual's need for privacy and storage space for personal grooming aids. Fixtures, cabinets, and equipment must be fitted carefully into limited space, and each bathroom function must be planned for.

Each year, suppliers and manufacturers come up with clever ideas for new and useful personal grooming products. Resourceful planning is often necessary when one tries to squeeze one more new item into an already overcrowded bathroom. Creating counter space and locating electrical outlets for such things as electric toothbrushes, curlers, and makeup mirrors takes ingenious scheming.

For those whose plans call for more than one bathroom, the questions in this bathroom section have been segregated according to the requirements for each individual bathroom. The bathroom serving the most bedrooms in the home has been designated "main bathroom," and the one serving the master bedroom has been designated "master bathroom."

The questions will alert you to the many factors to be considered when planning, equipping, and arranging space in these small areas. It is particularly important that you make decisions during the early stages of planning about the type and style of the bathroom fixtures you would like to have so that correct space allowances can be made for them.

When one is remodeling, the important task is to find modern fixtures that will fit into the spaces already available. A plumber's analysis of the plumbing already in the house and suggestions for connecting new fixtures would be valuable. If you plan to add a new bathroom, find out in advance what problem(s) there might be in connecting new piping and fixtures to the plumbing system already existing in the house.

If you will eventually require more bathrooms than you can presently afford, consider installing the rough plumbing (pipes in the walls) for the extra bathroom while your project is under construction so that plumbing fixtures can be conveniently and inexpensively added at a later time when you can afford to complete the extra bathroom.

When you have answered the following questions, you will have a clear picture of the kind of detailed preliminary planning necessary to create efficient, compact bathroom facilities that will serve your individual needs.

This is an important area of home planning — one where time invested in detailed planning will be extremely rewarding.

MAIN BATHROOM

1. DO YOU PLAN TO HAVE A MAIN, CENTRALLY LOCATED BATHROOM?

   _____

2. WILL THIS BATHROOM BE USED BY

   Family members?

       Adults _____ Occasionally _____ Often _____ Exclusively _____

       Children _____ Occasionally _____ Often _____ Exclusively _____

   Guests?

       Occasionally _____ Often _____ Exclusively _____

3. WHICH OF THE FOLLOWING TYPES OF FIXTURES SHOULD YOUR MAIN BATHROOM CONTAIN?

   A bathtub _____

   A shower over the bathtub _____

   A separate stall shower _____

   One basin installed in vanity cabinetry _____

   Two basins installed in vanity cabinetry _____

   A wall-hung basin without cabinetry _____

   A standard-type toilet _____

   A deluxe-type toilet _____

4. WILL ANYONE BE DRESSING IN THIS BATHROOM? _____

5. COULD YOU SAVE BATHROOM SPACE BY PROVIDING FACILITIES FOR APPLYING MAKEUP AND/OR FOR HAIR GROOMING IN BEDROOMS? _____

MASTER BATHROOM

6. DO YOUR PLANS CALL FOR A SEPARATE BATHROOM ADJACENT TO THE MASTER BEDROOM? _____

7. IF SO, WHO WILL USE THIS BATHROOM? _____

8. WHICH OF THE FOLLOWING TYPES OF FIXTURES SHOULD IT CONTAIN?

A bathtub _____

A shower over the bathtub _____

A separate stall shower _____

One basin installed in vanity cabinetry _____

Two basins installed in vanity cabinetry _____

One wall-hung basin without vanity cabinetry _____

A standard-type toilet _____

A deluxe-type toilet _____

A bidet _____

9. WILL ANYONE BE DRESSING IN THIS BATHROOM? _____

10. COULD YOU SAVE BATHROOM SPACE BY PROVIDING FACILITIES FOR APPLYING MAKEUP AND/OR FOR HAIR GROOMING IN THE BEDROOM?

_____

THIRD BATHROOM

11. WILL YOU NEED A THIRD BATHROOM? _____

12. IF SO, IN WHAT PART OF THE HOUSE SHOULD IT BE LOCATED?

Near the front entrance _____

Near the back or side entrance _____

Centrally _____

In another location _____

13. WILL THIS BATHROOM BE USED BY

Family members?

Adults _____ Occasionally _____ Often _____ Exclusively _____

Children _____ Occasionally _____ Often _____ Exclusively _____

Guests?

Occasionally _____ Often _____ Exclusively _____

14. SHOULD THIS BE A FULL BATH OR A HALF-BATH (One without bathing

 facilities)?_____

15. LIST THE FIXTURES IT SHOULD CONTAIN. _____

_____

_____

COMPARTMENTALIZED BATHROOMS

Bathrooms often function more efficiently and afford more privacy when they are compartmentalized. When the bathroom is to be used by two or more persons, it can be divided into compartments or areas to create private spaces within the main space. For example: the toilet — or the toilet and bathtub or shower — might be separated from the basin-vanity area. In some plans, the division is absolute, consisting of a wall and a door. In other plans, a visual barrier is erected, consisting of a partial wall or screen. In many plans, where there is a bathroom opening directly to the master bedroom, the basin and vanity area is open to the master bedroom. The bathing facilities and toilet in this type of plan are located in a separate closed compartment. Another alternative is a second basin in the basin-vanity compartment.

If your aim is to cut down on the number of bathrooms required, a compartmentalized plan might be the solution.

16. WOULD A COMPARTMENTALIZED BATHROOM SERVE YOUR FAMILY'S

 NEEDS? _____

17. WHICH BATHROOM(S) WOULD YOU COMPARTMENTALIZE? _____

18. WHICH FIXTURES WOULD YOU PLACE TOGETHER IN A SEPARATE

 COMPARTMENT TO DIVIDE THE BATHROOM?

 Toilet and basin with bathing facilities separate _____

 Toilet and shower or bathtub with basin separate _____

 Bathtub or shower and basin with toilet separate _____

19. *IF YOU ARE PLANNING A TWO-STORY HOUSE*

   Which bathroom(s) would be located upstairs? _____

   Which bathroom(s) would be located downstairs? _____

20. *WILL BATHING FACILITIES FOR AN INFANT BE NEEDED?* _____

21. *IF SO, WHAT LOCATION AND FIXTURE TYPE WOULD BE MOST SUITABLE?*

   _____

   _____

   _____

22. *WILL YOU NEED STORAGE IN THE BATHROOM(S) FOR ANY OF THE FOLLOWING THINGS:*

	Master Bathroom	Main Bathroom	Bathroom No. 3
Towels and other linens			
Soaps and paper supplies			
Cleaning supplies			
Medicines			
Grooming aids			
A hair dryer			
Hair curlers			
A makeup mirror			
A shaver			
A lather machine			
A toothbrush			
A Water-pik			
Other			

23. IF YOUR PLAN IS TO USE ANY OF THE PREVIOUSLY LISTED APPLIANCES, YOU WILL NEED A PLACE TO STORE AND USE THEM. WHAT FACILITIES WOULD BEST SUIT YOUR NEEDS? _____

_____

_____

_____

24. WHAT SPECIAL IDEAS DO YOU HAVE FOR BATHROOM HARDWARE SUCH AS

Towel bars? _____

Paper holders? _____

Grab-bars near the bathtub and/or toilet? _____

Medicine cabinet(s)? _____

Faucet and shower-head types? _____

Other hardware? _____

25. WHAT TYPE OF SHOWER DOORS AND/OR BATHTUB ENCLOSURE DO YOU PREFER

For bathtubs?

Waterproof curtains _____

Glass or plastic sliding doors _____

Plastic folding doors _____

For stall showers?

Waterproof curtains _____

Glass or plastic sliding doors _____

Glass or plastic hinge-type doors _____

Plastic folding doors _____

26. SHOULD YOUR BATHROOM WINDOWS BE

Translucent? _____ Clear glass? _____

27. WHAT OTHER IDEAS DO YOU HAVE FOR BATHROOM WINDOWS?

_____

_____

_____

28. DO YOU NEED ELECTRICAL OUTLETS IN THE BATHROOM(S) FOR ANY OF

THE FOLLOWING?

Small appliances _____ Jacuzzi for the bathtub _____

Heat lamp or wall heater _____ Exhaust fan _____

29. WHAT TYPE OF LIGHTING WOULD BEST SERVE YOUR NEEDS

In the toilet and shower or bathtub area? _____

Over the basin for shaving and grooming? _____

At a dressing table or makeup mirror? _____

30. DO YOU NEED A TELEPHONE JACK IN THE BATHROOM(S)? _____

31. DESCRIBE ANY TENTATIVE COLOR OR DECORATIVE WALL-TREATMENT

IDEAS YOU MAY HAVE FOR THE BATHROOM(S).

_____

_____

_____

32. DESCRIBE ANY FLOOR-COVERING IDEAS YOU MAY HAVE FOR THE

BATHROOM(S).

_____

_____

_____

33. WHAT IDEAS DO YOU HAVE FOR THE BATHROOM(S) THAT ARE UNIQUE TO YOUR LIFESTYLE? _____

_____

ALTERNATIVES:

If, in the final analysis, the budget must be cut, what alternatives would be acceptable to you? _____

_____

_____

COMMENTS AND REMINDERS: _____

_____

_____

_____

_____

_____

_____

_____

_____

_____

_____

_____

_____

_____

_____

THE BEDROOM SANCTUARY

Although the primary function of a bedroom is to provide a setting that is conducive to rest and sleep, it can also afford the opportunity for individual privacy, self-expression, and emotional growth. First consideration should be given to the location of the bedrooms in relationship to the overall plan. In order to select the most logical areas of the house for placement of bedrooms, it is important to think about sound control; analyze noise emanating from outside the home that will penetrate walls; noise from passing cars, from neighbors' houses, etc. If it is not possible to locate bedrooms in a quiet area, you may need to soundproof walls, double-glaze windows, and/or install heavy draperies to block out sound.

Another deterrent to rest is noise originating from within the home. It is often necessary to buffer such irritants as vibration and motor noise from appliances and equipment, footsteps on hard-surfaced flooring, voices, television, and stereo or radio.

When planning the location and use of bedroom space, keep in mind that most house plans are designed with bedrooms located in close proximity to each other and served by a central hall. Parents of infants and young children understandably prefer their children's bedrooms or nurseries to be close to their own. However, when formulating long-range plans, you may want to consider the possibility of locating the adults' bedrooms in a separate area from the children's bedrooms. Remember that small children will eventually be staying up later at night and they will be developing new interests, hobbies, activities, and friendships. Older children often prefer to use their rooms for such activities as entertaining playmates, listening to music, or watching television.

Another important factor in planning a restful setting is light control. Controlling light is often a simple matter of covering windows with shades, draperies, or louvers that can be adjusted to suit the sleeping habits of the room's occupant(s). Lighting plans should also include good arrangements for reading, grooming, etc.

It is seldom possible, when the family is large, to provide a separate room for each member. Sharing bedrooms can be a practical solution, particularly when each of the room's occupants takes part in the planning. Even small children can participate in the selection of such things as color, decorative treatment, and furnishings. If it is desirable to provide separate spaces within rooms, private areas can be created through strategic placement of storage cabinets, wardrobe closets, or screens.

The questions in this bedroom section call for decisions about the functional purposes that each of your bedrooms will serve and the facilities required for the performance of these functions. The person(s) who will occupy each room should participate in the planning of individual space(s). There is a separate page provided for analysis of the things required in each bedroom and also a page for each family member to express ideas and preferences about his or her "own space." A notebook can be used to supplement these pages if more writing space is needed.

1. *HOW MANY BEDROOMS DO YOUR PLANS CALL FOR?* _____

2. *HOW MANY OF THESE BEDROOMS WILL BE FOR ADULTS?* _____

   Will these rooms be shared by two or more persons? _____

3. *HOW MANY BEDROOMS WILL THERE BE FOR CHILDREN?* _____

   Will these rooms be shared by two or more persons? _____

4. *IN LOCATING BEDROOMS, WOULD YOU PREFER*

   All bedrooms to be served by a central hall? _____

   The adults' bedroom area to be separate from the children's bedroom area? _____

5. *DO YOU HAVE A SPECIAL LOCATION IN MIND FOR*

   A nursery? _____

   The bedroom of another adult family member? _____

   A guest room? _____

   A room for a live-in household helper? _____

   Other sleeping facilities? _____

6. *WILL BUFFERING OF SOUND FROM STREET NOISES BE A PROBLEM IN YOUR*

   LOCATION? _____

7. *IF SO, FOR WHICH BEDROOMS?* _____

   _____

8. *HAVE YOU ANY SPECIAL IDEAS FOR BUFFERING SOUND IN THE*

   BEDROOM AREA(S)? _____

   _____

   _____

   _____

   _____

   _____

ADULT'S BEDROOM AREA No. 1

Name(s) of person(s) who will occupy this bedroom.

_____

_____

1. WHERE SHOULD THIS BEDROOM BE LOCATED IN RELATIONSHIP TO OTHER AREAS OF THE PLAN? _____

_____

2. WHERE SHOULD IT BE LOCATED IN RELATIONSHIP TO THE LOT?

For best orientation to:

Sun _____ *View* _____

Bathroom _____

Noise emanating from outside the house _____

Noise originating from within the house _____

3. HOW MANY INDIVIDUALS WILL OCCUPY THIS BEDROOM? _____

4. IN ADDITION TO RESTING AND SLEEPING, WHAT OTHER FUNCTIONS MUST THIS ROOM ACCOMMODATE?

Dressing and storing clothing _____

Personal grooming and storing grooming aids _____

Studying or reading _____

Watching television _____

Listening to radio or stereo _____

Sewing _____

Other _____

_____

5. LIST YOUR IDEAS FOR SPACE AND STORAGE ARRANGEMENTS.

_____

_____

_____

6. SHOULD YOU PROVIDE ELECTRICAL OUTLETS FOR ANY OF THE FOLLOWING:

Lamps _____ Electric blanket(s) _____

Clock(s) _____ Radio _____ Television _____

Other appliance(s) _____

7. WHAT TYPE OF GENERAL ROOM ILLUMINATION DO YOU PREFER FOR THIS ROOM?

Ceiling lights(s) _____

Wall-mounted light(s) _____

Switched lamp(s) _____

   Controlled by:

      Regular switch _____

      Dimmer switch _____

      Delayed switch _____

8. WHAT SPECIAL IDEAS DO YOU HAVE FOR AREA LIGHTING, SUCH AS

Direct light on makeup mirror? _____

Reading lamps? _____

Bed lamps? _____

9. WILL YOU NEED A RECEPTACLE FOR A TELEVISION ANTENNA OR CABLE IN THIS BEDROOM? _____

_____

10. *DO YOU PLAN TO HAVE A TELEPHONE IN THIS BEDROOM?* _____

11. *DESCRIBE ANY TENTATIVE COLOR OR DECORATIVE WALL-TREATMENT IDEAS YOU MAY HAVE FOR THIS BEDROOM.*

_____

_____

_____

_____

12. *DESCRIBE ANY FLOOR-COVERING IDEAS YOU MAY HAVE FOR THIS ROOM.*

_____

_____

_____

_____

_____

ALTERNATIVES:

If, in the final analysis, the budget must be cut, what alternatives would be acceptable to you?

_____

_____

_____

COMMENTS AND REMINDERS:

_____

_____

_____

_____

ADULT'S BEDROOM AREA NO. 1
(continued)

Use this page to describe in detail, the bedroom space you would like to have for your personal use. Would it have lots of windows — a light, open feeling — or would it have smaller, draped or screened windows to create an intimate, cozy atmosphere?

_____

_____

_____

_____

_____

_____

_____

_____

_____

_____

_____

_____

_____

_____

_____

_____

_____

_____

ADULT'S BEDROOM AREA NO. 2

Name(s) of person(s) who will occupy this bedroom.

_____

_____

1. WHERE SHOULD THIS BEDROOM BE LOCATED IN RELATIONSHIP TO OTHER AREAS OF THE PLAN? _____

_____

2. WHERE SHOULD IT BE LOCATED IN RELATIONSHIP TO THE LOT?

For best orientation to:

Sun _____ View _____

Bathroom _____

Noise emanating from outside the house _____

Noise originating from within the house _____

3. HOW MANY INDIVIDUALS WILL OCCUPY THIS BEDROOM? _____

4. IN ADDITION TO RESTING AND SLEEPING, WHAT OTHER FUNCTIONS MUST THIS ROOM ACCOMMODATE?

Dressing and storing clothing _____

Personal grooming and storing grooming aids _____

Studying or reading _____

Watching television _____

Listening to radio or stereo _____

Sewing _____

Other _____

_____

5. LIST YOUR IDEAS FOR SPACE AND STORAGE ARRANGEMENTS.

_____

_____

_____

6. SHOULD YOU PROVIDE ELECTRICAL OUTLETS FOR ANY OF THE FOLLOWING:

Lamps _____ Electric blanket(s) _____

Clock(s) _____ Radio _____ Television _____

Other appliance(s) _____

7. WHAT TYPE OF GENERAL ROOM ILLUMINATION DO YOU PREFER FOR THIS ROOM?

Ceiling lights(s) _____

Wall-mounted light(s) _____

Switched lamp(s) _____

    Controlled by:

        Regular switch _____

        Dimmer switch _____

        Delayed switch _____

8. WHAT SPECIAL IDEAS DO YOU HAVE FOR AREA LIGHTING, SUCH AS

Direct light on makeup mirror? _____

Reading lamps? _____

Bed lamps? _____

9. WILL YOU NEED A RECEPTACLE FOR A TELEVISION ANTENNA OR CABLE IN THIS BEDROOM? _____

10. DO YOU PLAN TO HAVE A TELEPHONE IN THIS BEDROOM? _____

11. DESCRIBE ANY TENTATIVE COLOR OR DECORATIVE WALL-TREATMENT IDEAS YOU MAY HAVE FOR THIS BEDROOM.

_____

_____

_____

_____

12. DESCRIBE ANY FLOOR-COVERING IDEAS YOU MAY HAVE FOR THIS ROOM.

_____

_____

_____

_____

_____

ALTERNATIVES:

If, in the final analysis, the budget must be cut, what alternatives would be acceptable to you?

_____

_____

_____

_____

COMMENTS AND REMINDERS:

_____

_____

_____

_____

ADULT'S BEDROOM AREA NO. 2
(continued)

Use this page to describe in detail, the bedroom space you would like to have for your personal use. Would it have lots of windows — a light, open feeling — or would it have smaller, draped or screened windows to create an intimate, cozy atmosphere?

_____

_____

_____

_____

_____

_____

_____

_____

_____

_____

_____

_____

_____

_____

_____

_____

_____

_____

_____

_____

CHILDREN'S BEDROOM AREA NO. 1

Name(s) of person(s) who will occupy this bedroom.

_____

_____

1. WHERE SHOULD THIS BEDROOM BE LOCATED IN RELATIONSHIP TO THE PARENTS' BEDROOM? _____

    _____

2. WHERE SHOULD IT BE LOCATED IN RELATIONSHIP TO OTHER AREAS OF THE HOUSE? _____

    _____

3. WHERE SHOULD IT BE LOCATED IN RELATIONSHIP TO THE LOT?

    For best orientation to:

    Sun _____ View _____

    Play area _____Bathroom _____

    Noise emanating from outside the house _____

    Noise originating from within the house _____

4. HOW MANY INDIVIDUALS WILL OCCUPY THIS BEDROOM? _____

5. IN ADDITION TO RESTING AND SLEEPING, WHAT OTHER FUNCTIONS MUST THIS ROOM ACCOMMODATE?

    Dressing and storing clothing _____

    Personal grooming and storing grooming aids _____

    Playing and storing toys_____

    Entertaining playmates _____

    Homework or reading and storing books _____

Model-making or other handicraft and storing models or other "creations"

_____

Displaying collections _____

Storing athletic equipment and/or games _____

Watching television _____

Listening to radio or stereo _____

Other _____

6. *LIST YOUR IDEAS FOR SPACE AND STORAGE ARRANGEMENTS.*

_____

_____

7. *SHOULD YOU PROVIDE ELECTRICAL OUTLETS FOR ANY OF THE FOLLOWING?*

Lamps _____ *Electric blanket(s)* _____

Clock(s) _____ *Radio* _____ *Television* _____

Other _____

8. *WHAT TYPE OF GENERAL ROOM ILLUMINATION DO YOU PREFER FOR THIS ROOM?*

Ceiling lights(s) _____

Wall-mounted light(s) _____

Switched lamp(s) _____

   Controlled by:

   Regular switch _____

   Dimmer switch _____

   Delayed switch _____

_____

9. WHAT SPECIAL IDEAS DO YOU HAVE FOR AREA LIGHTING, SUCH AS

Direct light on makeup mirror? _____

Reading lamps? _____

Bed lamps? _____

10. WILL YOU NEED A RECEPTACLE FOR A TELEVISION ANTENNA OR CABLE IN THIS BEDROOM? _____

11. DO YOU PLAN TO HAVE A TELEPHONE IN THIS BEDROOM NOW OR AT SOME TIME IN THE FUTURE? _____

12. DESCRIBE ANY TENTATIVE COLOR OR DECORATIVE WALL-TREATMENT IDEAS YOU MAY HAVE FOR THIS BEDROOM. _____

_____

_____

_____

13. DESCRIBE ANY FLOOR-COVERING IDEAS YOU MAY HAVE FOR THIS ROOM.

_____

_____

_____

_____

_____

ALTERNATIVES:

If, in the final analysis, the budget must be cut, what alternatives would be acceptable to you?

_____

_____

CHILDREN'S BEDROOM AREA NO. 1
(continued)

Use this page to describe in detail, the bedroom space you would like to have for your personal use.

_____

_____

_____

_____

_____

_____

_____

_____

_____

_____

_____

_____

_____

_____

_____

_____

_____

_____

CHILDREN'S BEDROOM AREA NO. 2

Name(s) of person(s) who will occupy this bedroom.

_____

_____

1. WHERE SHOULD THIS BEDROOM BE LOCATED IN RELATIONSHIP TO THE PARENTS' BEDROOM? _____

   _____

2. WHERE SHOULD IT BE LOCATED IN RELATIONSHIP TO OTHER AREAS OF THE HOUSE? _____

   _____

3. WHERE SHOULD IT BE LOCATED IN RELATIONSHIP TO THE LOT?

   For best orientation to:

   Sun _____ View _____

   Play area _____Bathroom _____

   Noise emanating from outside the house _____

   Noise originating from within the house _____

4. HOW MANY INDIVIDUALS WILL OCCUPY THIS BEDROOM? _____

5. IN ADDITION TO RESTING AND SLEEPING, WHAT OTHER FUNCTIONS MUST THIS ROOM ACCOMMODATE?

   Dressing and storing clothing _____

   Personal grooming and storing grooming aids _____

   Playing and storing toys_____

   Entertaining playmates _____

   Homework or reading and storing books _____

Model-making or other handicraft and storing models or other "creations" _____

_____

Displaying collections _____

Storing athletic equipment and/or games _____

Watching television _____

Listening to radio or stereo _____

Other _____

6. LIST YOUR IDEAS FOR SPACE AND STORAGE ARRANGEMENTS.

_____

_____

7. SHOULD YOU PROVIDE ELECTRICAL OUTLETS FOR ANY OF THE FOLLOWING?

Lamps _____ Electric blanket(s) _____

Clock(s) _____ Radio _____ Television _____

Other _____

8. WHAT TYPE OF GENERAL ROOM ILLUMINATION DO YOU PREFER FOR THIS ROOM?

Ceiling lights(s) _____

Wall-mounted light(s) _____

Switched lamp(s) _____

    Controlled by:

        Regular switch _____

        Dimmer switch _____

        Delayed switch _____

_____

9. WHAT SPECIAL IDEAS DO YOU HAVE FOR AREA LIGHTING, SUCH AS

   Direct light on makeup mirror? _____

   Reading lamps? _____

   Bed lamps? _____

10. WILL YOU NEED A RECEPTACLE FOR A TELEVISION ANTENNA OR CABLE IN THIS BEDROOM? _____

11. DO YOU PLAN TO HAVE A TELEPHONE IN THIS BEDROOM NOW OR AT SOME TIME IN THE FUTURE? _____

12. DESCRIBE ANY TENTATIVE COLOR OR DECORATIVE WALL-TREAT-MENT IDEAS YOU MAY HAVE FOR THIS BEDROOM.

   _____

   _____

   _____

13. DESCRIBE ANY FLOOR-COVERING IDEAS YOU MAY HAVE FOR THIS ROOM.

   _____

   _____

   _____

   _____

   _____

ALTERNATIVES:

   If, in the final analysis, the budget must be cut, what alternatives would be acceptable to you?

   _____

   _____

CHILDREN'S BEDROOM AREA NO. 2
(continued)

Use this page to describe in detail, the bedroom space you would like to have for your personal use.

_____

_____

_____

_____

_____

_____

_____

_____

_____

_____

_____

_____

_____

_____

_____

_____

_____

_____

_____

CHILDREN'S BEDROOM AREA NO. 3 OR NURSERY

Name(s) of person(s) who will occupy this bedroom.

_____

_____

1. WHERE SHOULD THIS BEDROOM BE LOCATED IN RELATIONSHIP TO THE PARENTS' BEDROOM? _____

_____

2. WHERE SHOULD IT BE LOCATED IN RELATIONSHIP TO OTHER AREAS OF THE HOUSE? _____

_____

3. WHERE SHOULD IT BE LOCATED IN RELATIONSHIP TO THE LOT?

   For best orientation to:

   Sun _____ View _____

   Play area _____Bathroom _____

   Noise emanating from outside the house _____

   Noise originating from within the house _____

4. HOW MANY INDIVIDUALS WILL OCCUPY THIS BEDROOM? _____

5. IN ADDITION TO RESTING AND SLEEPING, WHAT OTHER FUNCTIONS MUST THIS ROOM ACCOMMODATE?

   Dressing and storing clothing _____

   Personal grooming and storing grooming aids _____

   Playing and storing toys_____

   Entertaining playmates _____

   Homework or reading and storing books _____

Model-making or other handicraft and storing models or other "creations" _____

Storing infant supplies _____

Displaying collections _____

Storing athletic equipment and/or games _____

Watching television _____

Listening to radio or stereo _____

Other _____

6. LIST YOUR IDEAS FOR SPACE AND STORAGE ARRANGEMENTS.

_____

_____

7. SHOULD YOU PROVIDE ELECTRICAL OUTLETS FOR ANY OF THE FOLLOWING?

Lamps _____ Electric blanket(s) _____

Clock(s) _____ Radio _____ Television _____

Other _____

8. WHAT TYPE OF GENERAL ROOM ILLUMINATION DO YOU PREFER FOR THIS ROOM?

Ceiling lights(s) _____

Wall-mounted light(s) _____

Switched lamp(s) _____

  Controlled by:

    Regular switch _____

    Dimmer switch _____

    Delayed switch _____

9. WHAT SPECIAL IDEAS DO YOU HAVE FOR AREA LIGHTING, SUCH AS

   Direct light on makeup mirror? _____

   Reading lamps? _____

   Bed lamps? _____

10. WILL YOU NEED A RECEPTACLE FOR A TELEVISION ANTENNA OR CABLE IN THIS BEDROOM? _____

11. DO YOU PLAN TO HAVE A TELEPHONE IN THIS BEDROOM NOW OR AT SOME TIME IN THE FUTURE? _____

12. DESCRIBE ANY TENTATIVE COLOR OR DECORATIVE WALL-TREAT-MENT IDEAS YOU MAY HAVE FOR THIS BEDROOM.

   _____

   _____

   _____

   _____

13. DESCRIBE ANY FLOOR-COVERING IDEAS YOU MAY HAVE FOR THIS ROOM.

   _____

   _____

   _____

   _____

   _____

ALTERNATIVES:

   If, in the final analysis, the budget must be cut, what alternatives would be acceptable to you?

_____

CHILDREN'S BEDROOM AREA NO. 3 OR NURSERY
(continued)

Use this page to describe in detail, the bedroom space you would like to have for your personal use.

_____

_____

_____

_____

_____

_____

_____

_____

_____

_____

_____

_____

_____

_____

_____

_____

_____

_____

_____

_____

A ROOM TO SERVE A SPECIAL PURPOSE

In analyzing your requirements you may find that conventional floor plans do not provide for an activity that is especially important to your family's way of life. If, after planning all the other rooms in your home, there remains an unfulfilled need for a room — to serve a special purpose — describe your requirements here.

1. *DO YOU NEED A ROOM FOR A SPECIAL PURPOSE?* _____

2. *WILL THIS SPECIAL-PURPOSE ROOM BE USED*

   As a study or library? _____

   As a den or television-viewing room? _____

   As an office at home? _____

   As a music room? _____

   As a guest room? _____

   As a children's playroom? _____

   As a sewing room? _____

   As a studio or workshop? _____

   As a hobby, recreation, or game room? _____

   Some other way(s) _____

3. *IN WHAT AREA OF THE HOUSE SHOULD YOUR SPECIAL-PURPOSE ROOM BE*

   LOCATED?

   In the bedroom area _____

   Near the front door _____

   Near or opening into a patio, garden, or deck _____

   Near the garage _____

   Other location _____

4. *IN THE FUTURE, MIGHT THIS ROOM SERVE A DIFFERENT PURPOSE?* _____

   _____

5. IF SO, DESCRIBE THAT PURPOSE HERE.

_____

_____

6. COULD A ROOM CONVENTIONALLY DESIGNATED "BEDROOM" BE CONVERTED TO FILL YOUR NEED? _____

7. BY WHOM WILL THE SPECIAL-PURPOSE ROOM BE USED?

Family member(s) _____ Guest(s) _____

8. DESCRIBE HERE ANY STORAGE OR DISPLAY FACILITIES REQUIRED.

_____

_____

_____

9. IS THIS A ROOM WHERE YOU WILL WANT LARGE OR SMALL WINDOWS?

(Consider the orientation of this room to the sun.) _____

10. WILL YOU WANT A PATIO OR A CONVENTIONAL DOOR IN THIS ROOM TO PROVIDE ACCESS TO A PATIO, TERRACE, OR DECK? _____

11. WHAT SPECIAL IDEAS DO YOU HAVE FOR THIS ROOM THAT ARE UNIQUE TO YOUR LIFESTYLE? _____

_____

_____

12. LIST ANY ELECTRICAL OUTLETS TO BE USED FOR SPECIAL EQUIPMENT IN THIS ROOM.

_____

13. WILL YOU NEED A RECEPTACLE FOR A TELEVISION ANTENNA OR CABLE IN THIS ROOM? _____

14. DO YOU PLAN TO HAVE A TELEPHONE IN THIS ROOM? _____

15. WHAT PLANS DO YOU HAVE FOR GENERAL ROOM ILLUMINATION AND/OR SPOT OR ACCENT LIGHTING? _____

_____

16. WHAT TYPE OF LIGHT SWITCHES DO YOU PLAN FOR THIS ROOM?

Standard _____ Dimmer _____ Switched lamps _____

17. DESCRIBE ANY TENTATIVE COLOR OR DECORATIVE WALL-TREATMENT IDEAS YOU MAY HAVE FOR THIS ROOM.

_____

_____

_____

18. DESCRIBE ANY FLOOR-COVERING IDEAS YOU MAY HAVE FOR THIS ROOM.

_____

_____

_____

ALTERNATIVES

If, in the final analysis, the budget must be cut, what alternatives would be acceptable to you?

_____

_____

_____

COMMENTS AND REMINDERS:

_____

_____

_____

_____

BASEMENT PLANNING

In some localities and under certain circumstances, basements are desirable and practical. In climates where frost penetration is deep and foundation footings extend below the typical frost line, basements are often designed and built as an integral part of the house. Under such circumstances, basements may provide economical space for housing mechanical equipment. Under optimum conditions, they may also provide additional living space.

In localities where weather conditions are more temperate and deep foundation walls are not required, or where the water table is high, basements are often undesirable.

NEW HOMES

1. DO YOU PLAN TO HAVE A FULL OR PARTIAL BASEMENT? _____

2. HAVE YOU INVESTIGATED YOUR LOT TO DETERMINE WHETHER THERE ARE

EXCAVATION PROBLEMS SUCH AS

Excessive rock or boulders under the topsoil? _____

An unusually high water table? _____ _____

3. DO YOU PLAN TO USE YOUR BASEMENT FOR ANY OF THE FOLLOWING

THINGS?

Housing heating or other mechanical equipment _____

Storing solar heat _____

For living space such as:

    A workshop _____

    A recreation room _____

    A laundry room _____

    A storage area for foodstuffs _____

    A general-storage area _____

4. *DO YOUR PLANS CALL FOR*

High windows for natural light and ventilation? _____

Wiring for electrical outlets and lighting? _____

Plumbing for a bathroom, sink, or laundry? _____

Partitions? _____

Other specifications? _____

REMODELING

5. *IS THERE A BASEMENT IN THE HOME YOU PLAN TO REMODEL?* _____

6. *IF THE BASEMENT IS TO BE CONVERTED TO LIVING SPACE, WILL IT REQUIRE*

Weatherproofing? _____

Ventilation, heat, and air conditioning? _____

Wiring for electrical outlets and lighting? _____

Plumbing for a bathroom, sink, or laundry? _____

Partitions? _____

Other changes? _____

7. *IS THERE ANY NATURAL LIGHT AVAILABLE IN THE EXISTING BASEMENT?*
_____

8. *IS THERE ANY NATURAL VENTILATION AVAILABLE?* _____

9. *IF NOT, HOW WILL YOU PROVIDE ADEQUATE LIGHT AND FRESH-AIR CIRCULATION?* _____

_____

10. *DESCRIBE HERE ANY PLANS YOU HAVE FOR REMODELING YOUR BASEMENT.*

_____

_____

_____

POOLS, HOT TUBS, SPAS, AND BATHHOUSES

More than 2 million families have installed their own above-ground swimming pools in the past ten years. Economical, above-ground swimming pools are making it possible for almost any family to enjoy the recreation and health benefits of swimming.

Above-ground pools are usually 4 feet in depth and come in sizes ranging from a circle with a diameter of 15 feet to an oval 20 by 40 feet. This type of pool comes in a kit form, usually consisting of steel or aluminum supports and walls with a liner made of heavy-duty vinyl, a pump, filter, and ladder; it can be installed in one day by two people using ordinary tools.

The more traditional, in-ground, pool is available in a variety of shapes and materials. There is an economical type which is similar to the above-ground pool; it also utilizes the vinyl liner. There are many other, more expensive types of in-ground swimming pools utilizing concrete or fiberglass.

Energy for pool heating is expensive and may soon be prohibitive. On warm days, pools gain heat because the surface of the water acts as a solar collector. Pool covers minimize heat loss by reducing or eliminating surface evaporation of heated water. New and specialized pool covers are now available. They increase the pool's capacity for collecting heat from the sun. For pools that must be heated, in the main, by some solar method, there are several effective solar pool-heating devices coming on the market.

The increased popularity of the redwood hot tub or the spa (a molded fiberglass variation of the hot tub) may be due to the high cost of heating a swimming pool. The hot tub and the spa are similar in operation. Most models simultaneously accommodate from 2 to 10 bathers who soak and relax in swirling water heated to a preselected temperature while water circulates through jet streams.

In the west, where hot tubs first became popular, bathhouses are often constructed outdoors as an adjunct to hot tubs. Since the use of the hot tub or spa has become popular throughout the country, indoor locations are more often chosen for installation (i.e., basements, recreation rooms, and oversized bathrooms) where they can be enjoyed all year long, without concern for the temperative outdoors.

SWIMMING POOLS

1. DO YOU PLAN TO INSTALL A SWIMMING POOL? _____

2. IF SO, WOULD IT BE INSTALLED

In the ground? _____

Above the ground? _____

3. IF A SWIMMING POOL IS TO BE INSTALLED IN THE GROUND

Is there access on your lot for excavation equipment? _____

How would you dispose of excess excavated earth? _____

4. ARE WATER AND ELECTRICITY AVAILABLE TO YOUR CHOSEN LOCATION?

5. HOW WILL YOU DISPOSE OF DISCHARGED WATER WHEN THE POOL MUST

BE DRAINED? _____

_____

6. WILL YOU WANT LIGHTING IN THE POOL OR AROUND THE POOL AREA?

_____

7. WHAT SAFETY PRECAUTIONS DO YOU PLAN TO TAKE?

Fencing to keep unsupervised children out of the pool area _____

Alarm bell _____ Life preservers _____

Other precaution(s) _____

8. WHAT OTHER PLANS DO YOU HAVE FOR YOUR SWIMMING POOL?

_____

_____

_____

_____

HOT TUBS OR SPAS

9. DOES A HOT TUB OR SPA FIT YOUR LIFESTYLE AND FIGURE IN YOUR

FUTURE PLANNING? _____

10. WOULD IT BE LOCATED INDOORS? _____ OR OUTDOORS? _____

11. IF OUTDOORS, WOULD YOU NEED A BATHHOUSE? _____

12. IF INDOORS, WHAT LOCATION WOULD YOU SELECT? _____

_____

13. *ARE WATER, ELECTRICITY, AND FUEL TO HEAT WATER AVAILABLE TO YOUR CHOSEN LOCATION?* _____

14. *WOULD YOU INSTALL THE HOT TUB OR SPA*

   In the ground? _____

   Partially in the ground? _____

   Below floor level (like a sunken bathtub)? _____

   At ground or floor level? _____

15. *WHAT SPECIAL IDEAS DO YOU HAVE FOR A HOT TUB, SPA, OR BATHHOUSE?*

_____

_____

_____

_____

_____

_____

_____

_____

_____

_____

_____

_____

_____

_____

PATIOS, COVERED TERRACES, AND DECKS

When the climate and environment of your setting are favorable to outdoor living, indoor spaces can be expanded visually as well as functionally by opening rooms to patios, terraces, or decks.

Decks are outdoor wooden platforms, constructed above ground, usually at — or close to — the level of the finished floor of the house. They are also used effectively on upper levels of split-level designs.

Decks are desirable in swimming pool, hot tub, or spa areas because decking is usually of smooth redwood or cedar that is naturally resistant to rot.

Dramatic effects can be achieved by building decks of varying heights, i.e., one deck at the floor level of the house and a connecting deck at the level of an above-ground swimming pool. When planter boxes of varying heights — and benches for seating — are constructed of decking materials, the effect is enhanced.

Patios or covered terraces can also be extremely useful and attractive. Cement paving with a smooth finish provides a durable and practical surface for a patio or terrace. Smooth cement surfaces are not only easy to clean, but suitable for recreational activities as well. They can be used for dancing, playing shuffleboard, and a host of other activities. Flagstones, cement with exposed aggregate, brick and other paving stones are all aesthetically attractive paving materials; but the rough textures inherent in each of these materials make them difficult to clean, and uneven surfaces make unsatisfactory floors for patio tables and chairs.

A patio or terrace that is roofed over with fiberglass, latticework, or some other light-filtering material becomes an area that is sheltered from direct sunlight and suitable for relaxing, dining, or entertaining.

A patio, covered terrace, or deck can be added very easily to an existing home. Facilities of this type contribute immeasurably to a home's attractiveness, comfort, and efficiency.

1. *DO YOU PLAN TO HAVE ANY DECK, PATIO, OR COVERED TERRACE AREAS?*

_____

2. *WHAT TYPE OF OUTDOOR FACILITIES DO YOU NEED?* _____

_____

_____

3. *WILL YOU NEED STORAGE FACILITIES NEAR THE PATIO, DECK, OR TERRACE AREA FOR SUCH ITEMS AS*

   Patio furniture? _____ *Cushions?* _____ *Games?* _____

   Portable barbecue? _____ *Other things?* _____

4. *WOULD OUTDOOR LIGHTING BE DESIRABLE SO THAT YOU CAN USE THESE FACILITIES IN THE EVENING?* _____

5. *WHAT IDEAS UNIQUE TO YOUR LIFESTYLE DO YOU HAVE FOR MAXIMIZING THE OUTDOOR LIVING POTENTIAL OF YOUR LOT?* _____*

   _____

   _____

ALTERNATIVES:

   If, in the final analysis, the budget must be cut, what alternatives would be acceptable to you for this space?

   _____

   _____

   _____

COMMENTS AND REMINDERS:

   _____

   _____

   _____

   _____

   _____

   _____

   _____

   _____

GARAGES, CARPORTS, DRIVEWAYS, AND PARKING SPACES

If you are hesitating between a garage and a carport, consider the severity of the weather in your locality, the number of items that must be stored in garage-type space, and the activities that will take place there. If your climate is mild, and your aim is simply to provide shelter for your car(s), a carport might be the right answer for you. Advantages of carports are that they cost less to build and they provide easy access and departure. Some disadvantages are the lack of protection from the elements and the unsightly look of stored items not in storage enclosures. If you opt for a garage, you will gain additional security and protection for your vehicles as well as extra storage and work space.

You who are remodeling may wish to convert garage space to living space. Often this is the most economical method of gaining additional living space, particularly if the existing garage is attached to the house.

Whatever your decision, an important factor in planning facilities for vehicles is design continuity between the garage or carport and the house. The garage takes up a large portion of the lot space and usually faces the street. It is important that the roof design be in keeping with the roof design of the house and that the garage door be harmonious with the finish materials used on the front of the house. If finish materials cannot be matched, they can, at the very least, be painted to blend and harmonize.

Automatic, remote-controlled garage-door openers cost much less than many other security devices and they have the added advantage of encouraging drivers to keep the garage door closed, thus providing additional security and eliminating the unsightly appearance of an open garage door.

The following questions will alert you to some of the many factors that should be considered when one is designing a garage or carport.

NEW HOME PLANNING

1. DO YOU PLAN TO BUILD A GARAGE FOR THE FAMILY'S CAR(S)? _____

2. WILL A CARPORT BE ADEQUATE? _____

3. SHOULD YOUR GARAGE OR CARPORT BE

An integral part of the house (attached)? _____

Separate from the house (detached)? _____

4. IF THIS FACILITY IS TO BE DETACHED, SHOULD IT BE ACCESSIBLE TO THE HOUSE

Through a breezeway or lanai (covered terrace or passage way)? _____

By a lighted pathway? _____

Through a courtyard? _____

Other means? _____

5. WILL THE GARAGE OR CARPORT BE LOCATED TO PROVIDE EASY ACCESS TO THE KITCHEN OR FOOD STORAGE AREA FOR CARRYING IN GROCERIES?

_____

6. IF YOU PLAN TO HAVE A CARPORT, WILL YOU NEED

Parking space for one car?_____two cars?_____

A storage locker or cabinets with doors to protect contents from the elements and help to maintain a neat appearance? _____

7. IF YOU PLAN TO HAVE A GARAGE, WILL YOU NEED

Parking space for one car?_____two cars?_____

8. WHAT ITEMS BESIDES CARS MUST BE STORED IN THE GARAGE?

Laundry equipment _____

A recreational vehicle _____

Camping equipment _____

A boat _____

Tools for garden or home workshop _____

Hobby, athletic, or sports equipment _____

Toys or games _____

Patio furniture and/or a barbecue _____

_____

9. WHAT TYPE OF STORAGE FACILITIES WILL YOU NEED FOR THE ITEMS PREVIOUSLY LISTED?

Shelving _____

Cabinetry _____

Describe other needs _____

10. WILL THE GARAGE BE USED FOR

Doing laundry? _____

Children playing? _____

Working on projects? _____

Repairing cars? _____

Other purposes or activities? _____

11. WHICH FAMILY MEMBER(S) IS MOST LIKELY TO USE THE GARAGE FOR A SPECIAL PURPOSE? _____

12. LIST ANY ITEMS YOU PLAN TO STORE IN THE GARAGE OR CARPORT AND THE SIZE OF EACH.

Description	Width (Side to side)	Depth (Front to back)	Height (Top to floor)

13. RECORD THE LENGTH AND WIDTH OF ANY VEHICLES YOU PLAN TO KEEP

IN THE GARAGE OR CARPORT.

Description	Width (Side by side)	Depth (Front to back)	Height (Top to floor)

14. DO YOU PLAN TO HAVE

A window for light and ventilation? _____

A door leading to the house? _____

A door leading to the garden? _____

15. DO YOU PLAN TO FINISH THE INTERIOR OF THE GARAGE?

Walls only _____ Walls and ceiling _____

16. IF AN OVERHEAD DOOR IS TO BE USED, WILL YOU INSTALL AN ELECTRIC,

REMOTE-CONTROLLED OPENER? _____

17. WHAT OTHER ELECTRICAL REQUIREMENTS DO YOU HAVE FOR THE

GARAGE OR CARPORT?

Lighting:

General illumination _____

Work area(s) _____

Outlets for:

Power tools _____ Electric lawn mower _____

Battery charger _____ Other equipment _____

18. LIST ANY OTHER IDEAS OR PLANS YOU HAVE FOR YOUR GARAGE OR CARPORT.

_____

_____

_____

_____

_____

_____

DRIVEWAYS AND GUEST PARKING SPACES

19. *WILL YOU NEED A PAVED DRIVEWAY OR APPROACH TO THE GARAGE OR CARPORT?* _____

20. *IF SO, SHOULD IT BE PAVED WITH*

    Concrete? _____

    Asphalt? _____

    Gravel? _____

21. *HOW LONG A DRIVEWAY WILL YOU NEED?* _____

22. *SHOULD THERE BE A PARKING AREA IN ADDITION TO THE GARAGE OR CARPORT SPACE FOR*

    Other family cars? _____

    Guest parking? _____

    A recreational vehicle? _____

REMODELING

23. *DO YOU PRESENTLY HAVE A GARAGE YOU WISH TO CONVERT TO LIVING SPACE?* _____

24. DESCRIBE YOUR PLANS FOR THIS NEW LIVING SPACE. _____

_____

_____

_____

_____

ALTERNATIVES:

_____

_____

COMMENTS AND REMINDERS:

SECTION

4

MAKING FINAL DECISIONS
AND
WRITING YOUR OWN SPECIFICATIONS

In Sections 1 through 3, each individual in the family has an opportunity to express ideas and preferences freely.

In Section 4, you will be making definite decisions and final selections. Numerous trade-offs may be necessary to consolidate ideas and achieve a plan that reflects the family lifestyle as a whole.

After general agreements have been reached by family members, you should shop for, investigate, price, and compare the many available types of materials and equipment. The charts in this section are for your use in listing specific choices, model numbers, brands, sizes, colors, etc. These completed pages can be removed from the book and referred to as plans for the home are being finalized.

A house is composed of a myriad of component parts, and each must work well with the others to form a cohesive whole. When decisions are being made about any single part, one must determine how well it serves the purpose and whether or not it fits the available space, the overall design concept, and the budget.

Specifications for installation of some items you select may call for work to be done during the course of construction. If you are building a new house, this preliminary work can often be accomplished more efficiently and with less cost if it is done while the house is being framed and before the walls are covered up. For example, correct space allowances and plumbing provisions must be made for bathtubs, showers, and toilets; selfcleaning ovens require venting; most clothes dryers have special electrical or gas and ventilation requirements; refrigerators with automatic ice makers must have water piped to them.

Decisions made before the project is under way will eliminate the necessity of giving spur-of-the-moment answers to contractors and workers while construction is being done. Selections made early should also eliminate the possibility of having to settle for substitutions because of the time element involved in obtaining an item or color on short notice.

If you discuss, plan, and verify each detail before construction begins, there is much less chance that expensive changes will have to be made after the project has begun. Changes made on the job often mean tearing out work, expense, frustration, and delay.

When the costs of the materials and equipment you have selected have been totaled, you will probably find that compromises must be made. It is sometimes possible to cut immediate costs by making any necessary preliminary provisions for special equipment or plumbing fixtures during the course of construction so that these items can be added at a later time.

Jot down your final decisions about each component part of the house on the charts in this section and list your selections. These simplified specification forms are easy to use and when completed will be invaluable to everyone concerned with your project.

FINAL DECISIONS
AND
SPECIFICATIONS

FOR:

Name(s) _____

Property address _____

And/or legal description _____

Telephone Number _____

ELECTRICAL APPLIANCES AND EQUIPMENT

	MAKE	MODEL	SIZE	COLOR
KITCHEN				
Range and oven combination (One-piece unit)				
Separate cooking top				
Separate wall oven(s)				
Single ☐				
Double ☐				
Self-cleaning ☐				
Continuous-cleaning ☐				
Standard ☐				
Exhaust fan or hood (over range)				
Exhaust fan for self-cleaning oven				
Range:				
Ceramic top ☐				
Electric-coil burners ☐				
Gas burners ☐				
Oven(s):				
Gas ☐ Electric ☐				
Microwave oven				
Barbecue				
Refrigerator				
Icemaker				

Freezer

Dishwasher

Garbage-disposal unit

    Installed in left-☐ or
    right-☐ hand sink

Trash compactor

Other appliance(s)

LAUNDRY AREA

Washing machine:

    Electric   ☐

    Gas   ☐

Dryer:

    Electric   ☐

    Gas   ☐

    Requires 220-volt
    electric outlet   ☐

    Requires venting   ☐

Door bell(s) and button(s)

Bell location:

    Front door   ☐

    Side door   ☐

    Back door   ☐

BATHROOM(S)

Exhaust fan(s)

Heater(s) room or space

Other _____

143

ELECTRIC LIGHT FIXTURES

INTERIOR LIGHTING

	MODEL	MAKE	COLOR
Inside entry			
Living room			
Family room			
Kitchen			
Dining area			
Laundry area			
Upstairs hall			
Stairwell			
Downstairs hall			
Main bathroom			
Master bathroom			
Bathroom no. 3			
Master bedroom			
Dressing area			
Bedroom no. 2			
Bedroom no. 3			
Bedroom no. 4			
Special-purpose room			
Garage			
Basement			

EXTERIOR LIGHTING

	MODEL	MAKE	COLOR
Front entry			
Back entry			
Side entry			
Garage entry			
Security lighting			
Other			

EXTERIOR FINISH SCHEDULE

EXTERIOR WALL FINISHES

Siding of: Stucco   ☐   Face brick or stone   ☐ _____

    Wood   ☐   Aluminum   ☐   Shingles   ☐

    Combined stucco and siding   ☐   Brick or cement block   ☐

    Other material(s) _____

ROOF COVERING

Shingles of: Wood   ☐   Slate   ☐   Ceramic   ☐

    Asphalt   ☐   Other material _____

    Fibrous glass roll roofing   ☐   Built up of tar and felt   ☐

Make of roofing material(s) to be used _____

    Type _____   ___   Weight _____   Color _____

COLOR SELECTIONS

Stucco _____

Siding _____

Masonry _____

Trim _____

Doors _____

Other areas _____

_____

_____

_____

_____

_____

FIREPLACES AND STOVES

MASONRY FIREPLACES OR BARBECUES

Location _____

Type and color of masonry surfacing material(s) to be used _____

_____

EFFICIENCY DEVICES

Air-circulating (convection) system such as the Heatolator brand _____

Glass doors installed in front of the firebox opening _____

Log lighter _____   Ash cleanout _____

METAL FIREPLACES

Make _____   Type _____

Model number _____   Color _____

Describe noncombustible material(s) to be used on, under, and/or near fireplace _____

_____

SPECIAL DESIGN TREATMENT

Mantle _____   Paneling _____   Other _____

_____

STOVES

Location _____

Describe _____

Make _____   Type _____   Model number _____

_____

_____

_____

FLOOR-COVERING MATERIALS

	TYPE	MAKE	STYLE	COLOR
Entry				
Living room				
Dining area				
Kitchen				
Laundry area				
Family room				
Main bathroom				
Master bathroom				
Bedroom no. 2				
Bedroom no. 3				
Bedroom no. 4				
Special-purpose room(s)				
Stairway(s)				
Hall(s)				
Other rooms or areas				

Describe pad, underlayment, or other materials required for installation of floor covering materials for each of the above choices _____

_____

_____

_____

_____

INSULATION AND WEATHER STRIPPING

INSULATION

Insulate ceiling with:

    Type of material to be used _____ Thickness _____

Insulate walls with:

    Type of insulation to be used _____ Thickness _____

Insulate ceiling with:

    Type of material to be used _____ Thickness _____

WEATHER STRIPPING

    Doors only   ☐   Doors and windows (if required for the type to be used)   ☐

    Type(s) of material(s) to be used _____

_____

_____

_____

_____

_____

_____

_____

_____

_____

_____

_____

INTERIOR FINISH SCHEDULE
FOR WALLS AND CEILINGS

	PAINT COLOR	TRIM COLOR	WALLS PAPERED	WALLS PANELED
Entry				
Living room				
Family room				
Kitchen				
Dining area				
Laundry area				
Upstairs hall				
Stairwell				
Downstairs hall				
Main bathroom				
Master bathroom				
Bathroom no. 3				
Master bedroom				
Dressing area				
Bedroom no. 2				
Bedroom no. 3				
Bedroom no. 4				
Special-purpose room				
Garage				
Basement				

LANDSCAPING, SPRINKLERS, PAVING, DECKING, AND FENCING

LANDSCAPING

Describe any landscaping to be done by others _____

_____

_____

SPRINKLER SYSTEM

Describe sprinkler system required and materials to be used _____

_____

_____

_____

PAVED AREAS

Describe size and shape of paved areas and paving materials to be used _____

_____

_____

_____

DECKING

Describe decking requirements _____

_____

_____

_____

_____

_____

_____

FENCING

Describe fencing requirements _____

_____

_____

_____

    Height of fencing required _____

    Gates required _____

    Materials to be used: Redwood ☐ Cedar ☐ Cement block ☐

    Chain Link ☐ Other _____

Describe requirements for other outdoor facilities _____

_____

_____

_____

_____

_____

_____

_____

_____

_____

_____

_____

_____

MECHANICAL EQUIPMENT

FURNACE

Make _____ Type _____ Model number _____

Capacity _____ Fuel required _____

Fuel storage tank or other facility required _____

AIR CONDITIONER

Make _____ Type _____ Model number _____

Capacity _____ Efficiency rating* _____

*(A higher efficiency rating means a lower operating cost.   Rating should be near 8.)

HOT WATER HEATER

Make _____ Type _____ Model number _____

Capacity _____ Fuel required _____

SPACE HEATER(S)

Make _____ Type _____ Model Number _____

Capacity _____ Fuel required _____

WATER SOFTENER

Make _____ Type _____ Model number _____

Capacity _____

Faucet for drinking water, not softened _____

OTHER MECHANICAL EQUIPMENT _____

_____

_____

_____

_____

MISCELLANEOUS   EQUIPMENT

List the rooms in which you want:

Television antenna or cable outlets _____

Telephone outlets _____

Intercom system _____

    Master station _____   Remote stations _____

Built-in vacuum-cleaning system ☐ Make _____   Model _____

Security devices:

    Burglar-alarm system ☐ Make _____   Model _____

    Smoke alarm ☐ Make _____   Model _____

List any other special electrical equipment or appliance(s) required:

_____

_____

_____

_____

SOLAR HEATING DEVICES

List and describe any devices to be used for solar heating _____

_____

_____

_____

_____

_____

_____

PLUMBING FIXTURES, FITTINGS AND ACCESSORIES

	FIXTURE	MAKE	MODEL	COLOR
Kitchen	Sink(s)			
Serving bar	Sink			
Laundry	Sink			
Main bathroom	Basin(s)			
	Toilet			
	Bathtub with shower over			
	Separate shower			
	Medicine cabinet(s)			
Master bathroom	Basin(s)			
	Toilet			
	Bidet			
	Bathtub with shower over			
	Separate shower			
	Medicine cabinet(s)			
Bathroom no. 3	Basin(s)			
	Toilet			
	Shower			
	Medicine cabinet(s)			

ACCESSORIES

List kitchen, serving bar, and laundry room fittings — such as faucets, towel bars, etc.

_____

_____

_____

List bathroom fittings such as shower heads, faucets and handles, grab bars, towel bars, paper holders, etc.

_____

List shower or bathtub enclosure type(s) or shower curtain rod required for each bathroom _____

_____

_____

List mirrors required for each bathroom _____

_____

_____

OUTDOOR PIPING AND/OR FAUCETS

List faucets required outdoors for:

Irrigation _____

Sprinklers _____

Pet area _____

Swimming pool, hot tub or spa _____

Hothouse (greenhouse) _____

_____

_____

_____

WINDOWS, SLIDING-GLASS DOORS, AND SPECIAL GLASS

List the type(s) and make(s) of windows required _____

_____

_____

List the type(s) and make of sliding doors required _____

_____

_____

Describe any special glass to be used:

    Decorative glass _____

    Peephole viewer _____

    One-way glass at front door _____

    Other _____

_____

_____

_____

_____

_____

_____

_____

_____

_____

_____

OTHER USEFUL BOOKS AND PUBLICATIONS

HOME PLANNING

DRAWING HOME PLANS-A Simplified Drafting System for Planning and Design...June Curran; Brooks Publishing Company, 930 Truxtun Ave., Suite 210, Bakersfield, CA 93301

ANATOMY FOR INTERIOR DESIGNERS...-Julius Panero; Whitney Library of Design, One Astor Plaza, New York, NY 10036

DESIGNING AND BUILDING A SOLAR HOUSE...D. Watson; Garden Way Publishing, Charlotte, VT 05445, 1977.

HOME LANDSCAPING

HOME OWNER'S GUIDE TO LANDSCAPE DESIGN...Timothy M. Michel; The Countryman Press, Taftsville, VT

PRACTICAL GUIDE TO HOME LANDSCAPING. Reader's Digest Association, Inc., Pleasantville, NY 10570

CONSTRUCTION FUNDS

OBTAINING CONSTRUCTION FUNDS-Where the Money Comes From...Don A. Halperin; John Wiley & Sons, 605 Third Ave., New York, NY 10016

HOME REMODELING

HOW TO REMODEL AND ENLARGE YOUR HOME...M. E. Daniels; Bobs-Merril, 4300 W. 62 St., Indianapolis, Ind 46206

REMODELING OLD HOUSES WITHOUT DESTROYING THEIR CHARACTER...George Stephen; Alfred A. Knopf, Inc., 201 E. 50 St., New York, NY 10022

HOME BUYING

HOME BUYER'S GUIDE...Jack Wren; Barnes & Noble, Inc., 10 E. 53 St., New York, NY 10022

SAVING ENERGY

DO-IT-YOURSELF INSULATION AND WEATHERSTRIPPING. A Sunset Book; Lane Publishing Company, Menlo Park, CA 94025

ENERGY FOR SURVIVAL...W. Clark; Doubleday & Co., Inc., New York, NY, 1974.

ENERGY PRIMER...Portola Institute; Whole Earth Truck Store, 558 Santa Cruz Ave., Menlo Park, CA 94025.

ENERGYBOOK #1: NATURAL SOURCES AND BACKYARD APPLICATIONS...J. Prenis (ed.); Running Press, Philadelphia, PA, 1975.

LOW-COST ENERGY-EFFICIENT SHELTER FOR THE OWNER AND BUILDER...E. Eccli (ed.); Rodale Press, Inc., Emmaus, PA 18049, 1976.

HOME ENERGY HOW-TO...A.J. Hand; Harper & Row, New York, NY 10022, 1977.

HOMEOWNER'S ENERGY GUIDE...J.A. Murphy; Thomas Y. Corwell Co., New York, NY 10003, 1976.

PUBLICATIONS

HUDSON HOME GUIDE, 289 So. San Antonio Rd, Los Altos, CA 94022.

BETTER HOMES AND GARDENS, 1716 Locust St., Des Moines, Iowa 50336.

HOUSE AND GARDEN, 350 Madison Ave., New York, NY 10017.

HOUSE BEAUTIFUL, 717 Fifth Ave., New York, NY 10020.

HOUSING, 1221 Ave. of the Americas, New York, NY 10020.

Co.EVOLUTION Quarterly, Box 428, Sausalito, CA 94965

MOTHER EARTH NEWS, Box 70, Hendersonville, N.C. 28739

SOLAR ENERGY *

Non Technical Books

THE COMING AGE OF SOLAR ENERGY...D.S. Halacy, Jr.; Harper & Row, Inc., New York, NY, 1973.

DIRECT USE OF THE SUN'S ENERGY...F. Daniels; Ballantine Books, Inc., Westminister, MD 1964.

THE SOLAR HOME BOOK...B. Anderson with M. Riordan; Cheshire Books, Harrisville, NH 1976.

SOLAR HOMES AND SUN HEATING...G. Daniels; Harper & Row, Inc., New York, NY, 1976

HOW TO USE SOLAR ENERGY IN YOUR HOME AND BUSINESS...T. Lucas; Ward Ritchie Press, Pasadena, CA 91103, 1977.

SOLAR AGE CATALOG...S. Oddo (ed.); Solar Age, P.O. Box 305, Dover, NJ 07801, 1977.

BUY WISE GUIDE TO SOLAR HEAT...F. Hickok; Hour House, P.O. Box 40082, St. Petersburg, FL 33743, 1976.

Periodicals

ALTERNATIVE SOURCES OF ENERGY. Alternate Sources of Energy, Inc., Route 2, Box 90A, Milaca, MN.

SOLAR AGE. Solar Vision Inc., P.O. Box 305, Dover, NJ 07801

SOLAR ENERGY. Pergamon Press Ltd., Maxwell House, Fairview Park, Elmsford, NY 10523

SOLAR ENERGY DIGEST. CWO-4 W. B. Edmondson, P.O. Box 17776, San Diego, CA 92117

SOLAR ENGINEERING. Solar Engineering Publishers, Inc., 8435 N. Stemmons Freeway, Suite 880, Dallas, TX 75247

SOLAR UTILIZATION NEWS. Alternate Energy Institute, P.O. Box 3100, Estes Park, CO 80517

*(Recommended reading list by the U.S. Department of Housing and Urban Development)